NOTES ON THE NAGA TRIBES

NOTES ON THE NAGA TRIBES

IN COMMUNICATION WITH ASSAM

JOHN OWEN

GYAN

Published by

Gyan Publishing House
5, Ansari Road
Daryaganj, New Delhi-110002
Phone: 011-47034999, 9811692060
E-mail: books@gyanbooks.com

Distribution Network
gyanbooks.com
India, USA, Canada, UK, Australia

ISBN: 978-93-6280-007-7 (PB)

First Published, 1844

2nd Impression 2025

Printed at: Gyan Press, Delhi.

NOTES ON THE NAGA TRIBES
Arthur: JOHN OWEN

NOTES ON

THE NAGA TRIBES,

IN COMMUNICATION WITH ASSAM;

BY

JOHN OWEN.

PUBLISHED BY REQUEST.

CALCUTTA:
W. H. CAREY AND CO., COSSITOLLAH,
1844.

THE

FOLLOWING PAGES

ARE DEDICATED TO

THE PRESIDENT AND MEMBERS

OF

The Royal Geographical Society of Great Britain,

BY

THEIR FAITHFUL SERVANT,

THE AUTHOR.

PREFACE.

THE preface, to one unaccustomed to the pains and honours of authorship, is perhaps the most difficult part of his labours. The present work is one that will blush to find a name, for it was begun only as a rough detail of facts, that occurred within the writer's personal observation, and is only cast on the world at the persuasion of a few friends, partial ones no doubt, who considered that some of them were novel, and therefore worth the communicating, if only as feelers for the publication of the movements of those more able than the author of the present *brochure*.

But at all events; the filling up of his original sketches has served to amuse vacant hours; which have been unwillingly obtained, as they would be joyfully relinquished, could he find any more profitable means of employing them.

If the following notes should develope or assist the inquiries of others, or serve to wile away a spare portion of time with the passing reader, his wishes are more than gratified, and he will for once think that he has not quite wasted his time. It will be evident to many readers, that, where necessary, the writer has not hesitated to avail himself of the observations of others on the same tract of country, and particularly of those of Mr. Robinson, who has been more fortunate than himself in having had access to public documents which were not available upon the present occasion. To this gentleman, therefore, are tendered the best acknowledgements for the use made of his observations.

HISTORY OF THE

NAGA TRIBES IN COMMUNICATION WITH ASSAM.

Those tribes known generally as Nagas, inhabit mountainous districts on the upper part of the valley of Assam, and southward of the Brahmapootra, not extending higher north than to a tributary of that great river, known as the *Boree Deehing*, in a latitude of about 17° 15'. The whole line of these tribes, which pursues a north-easterly and south-westerly direction, embraces perhaps some fifty or sixty independent chieftainships, bounded on the south by an imaginary line near the 23rd degree of latitude; on the north by the plains of Assam; on the east by the Bor Kampti ranges, and principal source or feeder of the Kiayn-dcayn alias Thanla-waddy; and on the west by the eastern frontier of Tipperah. But of these races, generally, little is known; those whom it is intended to describe, being "Nagas in communication with Assam," and amongst the principal are the *Nam-Sangeeas* or *Kang-jangeeas*, the *Bur-dwarreeas* or *Takumeeas*

Boundaries of the Naga ranges.

and the *Pannee dwarreeas* or *Bur-gyahs.* These three tribes now in communication together inhabit mountains proximate to, and connected, yet independent of one another—rising gradually from the adjacent plains to the height of three and four thousand feet above the level of the sea. The superficial extent on which these mountains rest does not occupy more than a hundred and forty or fifty square miles, bounded on the north by the Boree Deehing, which separates them from the Singphoes, eastward by the Abors, and Bor Abors, south by the Banphera Nagas and westward by the plains of Assam between Jaipoor and Bursully. The Abor ranges increase in height towards the Burmah frontier to eight and ten thousand feet, appearing on a clear day to terminate in blue conical or broken summits, and affording as may be imagined a most imposing appearance.

As the habits and customs of these three tribes assimilate in nearly every respect, it will be unnecessary to treat on them separately—further than to show the geographical position of each clan, and the different vegetable and mineralogical resources existing on certain hills only.

Description of Country. Claiming little or no interest for the capitalist beyond its forests of indigenous Tea, this section of the hills presents many subjects for enquiry equally interesting to the geographer, the observer of the human races, and the lover of research; for while its scenery invites the stranger to visit its mountain falls and its gorgeous summits, the change of atmosphere on the heights invigorates and leads him, in the months of December and January, to the happy but delusive belief of imagining himself in the temperate regions of the more western Himalaya.

The labyrinth of crystal streams pursuing their passage in every direction, through glens and ravines, to some fall or basin, from whence struggling towards the plains, they feed the tributaries of the great Bramahpootra; and the display of wild vegetation, mountains, hills, and dales, clothed with forests of the most luxuriant foliage, the birds'-eye view of which from some towering summit, cannot but afford enthusiastic delight to the contemplating spectator.

Derivation of the word Naga.

The word "*Naga*," (a Sanscrit one) appears to be identical with "snake"—whence perhaps *Naja*, applied by Zoologists to the Cobra or hooded snake; for, on the authority of a good Sanscrit scholar, it may be translated not only into a snake, but a swiftly travelling one too, a derogatory term applied in all probability by the natives of the plains to them, from their notoriously shy, stealthy habits, and wandering life. Not recognizing the word themselves, makes it the more probable, as they themselves distinguish one another by other appellations, noticed at the head of this chapter.

Periodical inundations.

During the periodical inundations, the scenery of course becomes somewhat changed; rain so plentifully bestowed and so little courted in this latitude floods the little mountain torrents; the ravines fed by passing rivers necessarily fill, and their waters carry away in their progress whatever opposes them, tearing away gigantic trees from their roots—stones of immense size—and even forcing rocks from the centre of their beds. It is then that this charming spot becomes divested of its beauty; and its character, heretofore famous for salubrity, is entirely converted, by being rendered dangerous to the European constitution under the noxious exhalations engendered by surrounding decayed vegetation, not only on the lower grounds, but where inundation does not actually reach; the fall of moisture, and its accumulation in the dense forests creating as a necessary consequence unwholesome vapours and death-dealing malaria.

Fevers not prevalent amongst them. The malignant fevers which are so prevalent amongst the natives of the plains, to the Naga are almost unknown. Whether this arises from their sturdy frames, habitual exercise in their agricultural pursuits, or the absence of exciting causes, such as the almost total disuse of opium, until of late, is a matter of little moment. The fact is beyond doubt;—still it has been found that the Assamese are not equally fortunate in this more wooded but less marshy spot.

Rains. The cessation of the rains, as in most tropical countries, is supposed to be the most unhealthy season of the year, which as elsewhere in Bengal is generally found from the middle of August to the end of September.

From June to August the Nagas and Assamese have little communication with one another, occasioned by the impossibility of crossing mountain torrents. It is then that the Naga depends entirely on the forest for his subsistence, gathering to satisfy his appetite, roots of trees, wild yams, and other vegetable productions. Animal food such as the deer, wild buffaloe, or other forest *janwar*, is difficult to procure, from the same cause; and if mortality be ever prevalent on these hills, it is owing to virulent dysentery engendered by exposure and want of nutritious food.

North-westers.

North-westers are common during the months of April, May, and June, and are severely felt on the bleak summits by the Nagas; the poorer class of whom are frequently known on such occasions, that they may obtain warmth, to plaister their bodies all over with mud. Certain atmospheric changes warn him of their approach, when those engaged in any kind of work near to forests, fly to those villages free from jungle, for security; gigantic trees, overtopping all their surrounding ones, on these occasions are frequently torn up by the roots, and falling on those beneath them, the work of destruction commences, burying elephants, buffalos, and other animals under their tremendous weight. These North-westers generally commence at sunset, and before the dawn of day nature smiles again in all her loveliness.

Mist. The absence of mist, which in the winter prevails so universally in Assam, is rather an extraordinary fact, but not the less acceptable, abounding as these hills do in vegetation.

Temperature. The mean annual temperature is about 64—the thermometer in the winter keeping steady at 49, and in the summer months at about 80.

Dropsy, Elephantiasis, &c. No one single instance of either dropsy, elephantiasis or asthma has ever presented itself, to afford a belief of its existence, amongst them. Their athletic exercises, continual ascents and descents, moreover, forbid the assumption.

Cholera. Cholera makes its appearance at times, but not in a fatal form. Immersion in water is strangely enough imagined by them to be a remedy ; but subsequent cures by other more real treatment, such as an administration of opium and brandy, which, at once arresting the disease, has shewn them the fallacy of their former belief.

Small-pox. None are marked with small-pox, nor do they even know the disease ; but scorbutic eruptions on the body are common, arising perhaps from exposure to wind and weather.

Descent. Any attempt to account for their descent without an intimate knowledge of their dialect, would be as difficult as absurd. Still the similarity of features, habits, language, and practices, bespeaks them to be of one common origin, from whatever part of Asia they emigrated, which is evident, as no one neighbouring tribe bears a corresponding feature to them. Both Singphoe, Kampti, Bhooteea, Meeree, Duphla, and others, are of a totally different form and stamp, devoid of the distinguishing wild expression which so prominently characterises them. Various opinions prevail, some of which are, speaking of them generally, that "the aborigines fled from the north-west borders of China, probably during the sanguinary conflicts for supremacy which took place between the different members of the Chinese and Tartar dynasties in the thirteenth and fourteenth centuries; others may from like political causes have been driven into the fastnesses of these hills from Assam and Bengal, and brought with them languages very different from each other."

Annexation of this territory to British Indian Dominions desirable.

The annexation of the whole line of these races to our British Indian dominions, although many of them were always supposed to pay allegiance to the sovereigns of Assam, would be, if treated for in an harmonious manner, highly desirable, as affording to our frontier a natural barrier from Burmese invasion. That they should have paid allegiance to the Rajahs in former times, was imperative from the absence of grain in their own hills, and the profitable barter with salt, for that commodity—manufactured by them from their own brine springs.

Taxes on Salt.

"The taxes that have been until lately levied on the Naga salt, have been exceedingly heavy, and the manner in which they were imposed led to numerous exactions on the part of the tax-gatherers. The individuals appointed to the collection of the taxes were in attendance at the springs on the hills as well as the markets below, and tolls were levied by them, both on the salt itself and on the articles the Nagas obtained in barter for the salt."

Since abolished. These taxes have been abolished, and the British government no longer exercise any prerogative in their claim to these springs; many of them, it is to be regretted, were filled up by the Nagas, and in such a manner as to prevent the possibility in most cases of future access. An account of their manufacturing process will elsewhere be found.

Religion. It has been asserted, and is generally admitted in the plains of Assam, that the Nagas have no religion—which will undoubtedly bear a contradiction, for, in common with many savage tribes who worship some particular orb either of day or night, so it is with the Naga, who imagines the sun to be his presiding deity. Should any of their tribe meet a sudden death, the body is that instant committed to the flames, such party, according to their idea, having incurred the displeasure of the deity.

Moreover, the existence of a singular practice amongst them negatives the idea of their being without religious feelings, for to what can we ascribe the following observance if it be not intended as devotional. At every cross-path they meet on a march, each, whether man, woman, or child, breaks off a branch or leaf of a tree which is thrown on a heap whilst passing—and these continue accumulating until an eclipse takes place, when the whole are removed by fire. The motive for so strange a practice I could never ascertain, with any nearer approach to correctness than my interpreter's knowledge could afford me, viz. that their Supreme One might see their observance, and reward them accordingly. But putting on one side this explanation of the custom, which, in all probability, being an Assamese, he did not take the trouble to enquire into minutely—it is evidently an act of religious respect which is sufficient to confute the hitherto acknowledged absence of all religious feeling on the part of the Naga tribes.

Missionary labor.

Missionary labors have proved sorely unproductive, although the Reverend Mr. Bronson, an American Missionary, compiled a small vocabulary with a view to establish a school for the education of the children. The novelty at first created uncommon inquisitiveness. Younger branches of their families intimated a desire to read and learn, but all interest ceased on finding, after some days, a discontinuation of the presents that had been given in the first instance to win their attention—such as beads, looking-glasses, and other baubles.

Visits from foreign tribes

Each class being governed by independent chieftains, they see but few strangers, and these not of frequent occurrence. are principally *Mohungeeas*, or Assamese traders from the plains, who, with a view to obtain salt, carry up for barter quantities of grain and opium, together with a few cocks, as a present for the Khoonbow or chief. It is a singular fact that they have such an aversion to the flesh of any female, as, in the absence of those of the male kind, to refuse this description of food altogether. They however eat of fish, snakes, &c. without endeavouring to make the same distinction.

Manner of cooking generally. Their manner of cooking is performed in joints of bamboos, introduced into which are as much rice, chillies, and flesh, with water, as each will hold, all mixed together and thrust tightly in by the aid of a stick; a couple of bamboos placed in the ground, with a third connecting them at the top horizontally, constitutes a fire-place, against which those holding the food rest; by continual turning it soon becomes well roasted without splitting the bamboos, a circumstance which rarely occurs, and served up on leaves from any neighbouring tree, they sit down to their simple repast with as much real enjoyment, as those of more civilized habits.

In their domestic state they are often found in a state of nudity. In their domestic condition, both sexes on many of the hills are found in *puris naturalibus*; but before the Assamese, who are generally well clothed; if possessed of a piece of cloth they will wear it. No people perhaps in the world are more alive to the preservation of matrimonial honor than the Nagas, and any offer of insult to the wife or daughter of another, would meet with deadly satisfaction from either the battle-axe or spear.

As compared with the more refined Assamese, their dwelling-houses and appurtenances appear filthy in the extreme, and the farm-yards under their houses, which are supported on posts or bamboos, are none of the cleanest. Still, many of them are remarkably neat, and display a degree of care in the interior arrangements seldom the case with their Eastern neighbours. Thatched with *Toka Pat*, a very large leaf indigenous to their hills, and the sides covered with mat, grass, and mud, their houses are rendered impervious to wind and rain; each has generally three different apartments, which are respectively appropriated to the purposes of sleeping, cooking, and general business. Having no windows, the smoke escapes through the roof and doors, which answer two purposes—the preservation of the thatch, and impossibility of their manufactured salt becoming injured. Vessels of any kind are not eagerly sought for by them, the bamboo answering every purpose. Large mats made of the aforenamed leaves constitute their sleeping-places, which, in wet weather, placed near a large fire, continually kept up in the chamber, is not an uncomfortable place of rest.

Description of their dwelling-houses.

The unmarried men are not allowed under any consideration to sleep at night in the family residence—as will hereafter be noticed.

Hospitality. They are extremely hospitable according to their own method, and after a little mutual accommodation, are ever ready to relieve the wants of a traveller by the offer of house, village supplies, and attendants.

Human skulls form the principal ornament of a chief's residence. What strikes the stranger most on entering a chief's residence is the collection of skulls, both human and of the field, slung around the walls inside. Here repose heads of chieftains slain in battle, or perhaps coaxingly seduced—from some wrong, real or imaginary—with a view to settlement, and too often treacherously murdered. The following is an instance;

An instance of Naga treachery. Unglee-Cut—so called by the Assamees from having had one of his fingers removed for committing some error, while premier to the chieftain, or *Bur Khoonbow*—hearing that *Bangoneea*, one of *Dant Seegah's* sons, designated also as tooth-broken, was proceeding on an excursion to the Abor ranges, sent to him with a plentiful promise of presents, desiring the messenger to express his deep sorrow that their quarrels should have remained so long unadjusted, merely on account of a few villages, and requested an interview on a certain hill, to which place he would dispatch empowered parties to meet and settle all differences. On Bangoneea's approach to the appointed place, he was surrounded and treacherously murdered, with a number of his followers, by people who had lain in ambush for them.

Happily such records of crime are now less numerous, corrected by the interference of our Government, which has promised protection, on the understanding that all causes of grievance be referred to its officers.

Value of iron in their estimation.

There is an extraordinary value attached to iron by these hardy mountaineers, and they appear with manly pride to think the article to have been discovered, and brought into the shape of weapons, only for warriors.

Instruments of war.

Their instruments of war are the battle-axe, of which there are three kinds; the handles, two feet in length, covered with a jet black varnish, hold the different shaped blades. The spear, which is of an usual size, is ornamented with goat's hair, dyed in *Munjeeth*, and further embellished with narrow strips of rattan, of various hues. The shield, three and a half feet long and two feet broad, of a triangular shape, and lined with mats, is impenetrable to the spear and battle-axe, but far from being ball-proof.

It is a curious fact that they do not, like all their neighbours, use the bow and arrow; this distinguishes them as being of an entirely different race from all the others, and assists in tracing them from Tartary or China, rather than from Bootan;—for, this fatal instrument, when poisoned with *Be*, a Mishmee herb, deals in the hands of a Singphoe active death around. Such a value do the Nagas attach to their daws and spears, that one would almost imagine them to have been consecrated by some great unknown. The battle-axe is his companion whether asleep or awake, in sanguinary conflict, in his agricultural pursuits, and in the domestic exercise of making a basket, or shaping out a wooden ornament.

Precaution from attack by planting on the approach poisoned pieces of bamboo.

In expectation of an attack they collect strong slips of bamboos which they cut into lengths of eight and ten inches, and finely point either end, one of which is impregnated with the fatal *Be*, while the other is inserted in the ground amongst the grass, near the approach to the village, where it is imperceptible to the eager invader. Along the passes they are likewise planted, and as the cautious Naga crouches to the place of attack in the depth of night, one by one falls to the ground and meets instantaneous death, with little if any suffering. This stratagem is invariably resorted to.

Also by blocking up the roads to prevent ingress.

The more timid, and inhabitants of less populated villages, in anticipation of danger, to prevent the enemy's approach, knock down all the trees on each side of the pathway, leading from the main one to the village—so as effectually to block up all chance of ingress; and so cunningly is this executed, that in many cases, although the enemy may be well acquainted with the neighbourhood, they become so perplexed by the delay, as to find the day dawn, when they fly to the forests, and often superstitiously fear to renew the attack.

Both sexes in some instances delight in ornamenting their naked bodies with rattan, amber, and glass beads. And the warriors, with the addition of human hair, strings of teeth extracted from the jaws of their fallen enemies—tusks of boars as ear-rings, wear a hideous warlike aspect—the greater part of which articles remain on them working, bathing, and sleeping.

Articles of ornament for their bodies.

A remarkable feature in the Naga is the deficiency of hair. On the face it is seldom or ever found—either in the shape of beard, whisker or moustache, and on the head it is deficient in quantity, is knotted on the crown, and fastened with a rude semi-circular comb, manufactured by themselves either from the wood of the *Jack*, or the *Tetahapa*. The average height of them is about five feet ten inches and they are seldom inclined towards obesity.

Hair not abundant on the persons of the Nagas.

Their manner of putting to death a wild ox or buffalo is as barbarous as novel. The animal is fastened to the stump of a tree, house-post, or other secure holding-place, by rattans passed through the nostrils—the warriors of the village surround it, and on the chief approaching, all utter a shrill piercing cry, with the intention of stupifying it, when the head man, advancing from behind, hamstrings, and very often severs at one blow the leg in halves, under the joint. It is immediately knocked down, the spine bone separated in an instant into innumerable pieces—spears dance in the body—wild hal-

Mode of killing oxen, buffalos, &c.

loos echo in the distance,—and the display of savage delight on such an occasion, is not perhaps in any part of the world to be equalled. Literally alive, so far as the muscular action of the flesh is perceptible, the several parts are torn from the body and borne away to their respective habitations. But this is not the most animated part of the scene—if animation it be—for immediately the hacking commences, *choongas* or joints of bamboos are placed by the multitude at each incision, with the view of catching the blood, using while warm the same as an actual bedaubment for their persons. To the spectator unaccustomed to such scenes, the exhibition is a fearful one, while the passions of the excited Naga become to an extensive degree overbearing and disgusting. Dances, sham fights, follow, and but too often mirth is speedily converted into deadly combat.

Mode of cooking the same.

But the sun sets—individuals are seen collecting into groups, each having brought with him from the neighbouring forest some huge tree or load of firewood, which one would have imagined a human being scarcely capable of bearing. The whole is collected in a pile and fired; the *Nagonees* (their females) bring their portions, join, and preparations are made for cooking the flesh, which, by the bye, the writer was rather surprised at witnessing, taking into consideration their savage-like preliminaries. The skin is not removed, but the flesh, cut into two or three-ounce pieces, is thrown amongst the ashes at the foot of the fire;—the hair, scarcely singed, is removed from it, and with the addition of a forest yam, or wild kind of potato, the repast commences, occasionally varied by a song or war-dance. As buffalo meat is an unusual, or rather not common, entertainment amongst them the festivities are prolonged to beyond midnight; the men, as of other countries, to promote mirth freely partake of an intoxicating drink distilled from rice—and overcome by its effects, instead of retiring to their habitations, they sleep around the fire—not, in the cold weather, an unenviable place of rest.

The compiler of these notes would consider that, supported as he has been, by that enterprising body of merchants—"THE ASSAM COMPANY"—he would commit an act of injustice were he to omit recording any information that would be of service to them, his chance of obtaining every acquaintance connected with these particular Nagas having been, strictly speaking, at their expense. He would therefore suggest, that on the discovery and purposed clearing of an indigenous tea tract on these hills, every possible invitation should be encouraged. Assam Tea Company.

Other suggestions may be introduced as they occur—but the foregoing subject led to the idea—that on such occasions, from the fact of their love of forest incendiarism, the Nagas are really useful auxiliaries towards *clearances*—in- Nagas useful auxiliaries to them.

dependent of the smart smash they can when willing, exercise in the jungle, and when entertained in the day time on pay, or remuneration as labourers with their ever-ready-toned weapons.

Mode of swearing to keep the peace.

Their both rude, and singular method of swearing to keep the peace with one another is on record, and deserving of notice. Each chief, supplied with a dog and a few cocks, meets at a *Morang*, or village hall, in presence of their respective warriors and a large assembly of villagers. At a signal from the administrar of the oath, with one blow from the battle-axe each dog's head is severed from the body, and the blood, stirred up with the forefinger beforehand, is thrown on their weapons, by which they pledge themselves to suffer death, rather than break the peace. The birds form flesh for a repast, after which a mutual good understanding is supposed to exist. Such fact is on record, and brought to notice by our Government having sent a deputation to the *Nam Sangeea* and *Bur-dwareea* chiefs, between whom incessant quarrels were taking place, detrimental to the preservation of tranquillity on our frontier.

Hunting.

Hunting forms a favourite amusement with them, and the flesh of the elephant is esteemed a delicacy. It is captured by them entirely through stratagem. A large hole, capable of receiving it, is dug on a track-way, covered over with a little grass and earth. They then trace it, and with screams and shouts frighten it back, but although the animal is sufficiently sagacious to see its trap, not being able to get into the jungle on either side of the track with ease, in its fright, trumpeting alarm, plunges headlong into it, and is thus secured. As in the murdering of a buffalo, so is it with the elephant—spears pierce the body, the trunk raised in agony is separated with the battle-axe, and thus is this noble animal, powerless, left to expire by loss of blood—when it is taken from the pit in pieces and carried to their villages. Sometimes they capture males with tusks weighing half a maund each, which are disposed of to the *Marwarrees*, merchants of the plains, for the exchange of a few beads and shells.

Their dogs have a peculiar dexterity in catching deer for them. They go out into the woods at day-break, set together on one or more, which they kill, return home, making the circumstance known by a continual howling, with an inclination to return, when the delighted Naga follows them in the rear, and if a tiger has not been in the way he soon finds the slain, and at once removes it to his habitation. The stratagem rarely fails, and the dogs never leave until they are satisfied of actual death.

Nagas seldom marry into other tribes and in this instance for powerful alliance only.

Except in one or two instances, the Naga people have not been known to associate in marriage with any others, or even between tribe and tribe; the exceptions having been invariably with a view to strengthen the power of their own tribe by a foreign alliance that shall insure it the assistance of some powerful neighbouring chief. They are not usually contracted until both parties have reached the age of puberty—few instances of earlier betrothal having been known; at the same time a difference of opinion prevails as to the form of contract, although in either way little solemnity is exhibited.

The writer's opinion of the ceremony.

In the writer's opinion the following is the generally accepted marriage ceremonial, so to speak—primitive it is true, nevertheless characteristic of this people. Chance of course never permitted him the opportunity of watching a pair through the tedious period of courtship, but they elope together for this purpose, to some wild retreat, where all fear of pursuit is out of the question. After the expiration of three or four days, they return to their respective families and if each be satisfied with the other the marriage is consummated; but if, during the period of this wild suit, any impropriety on the part of the lovers should have been detected by the parents, both suffer by order, instant decapitation. Should, however, mutual satisfaction be wanting, the young people are allowed to make other selections, and the former unsuccessful attempt is scarcely considered worthy even of mention in conversation. The principal part of the ceremony, as in all others, amongst these in common with the general races of mankind, consists in feastings and rejoicings, and hence arises a disinclination on the part of a Naga to marry a man who may not have it in his power to afford a suitable entertainment.

An officer in his report to Government on what he saw amongst these people writes— An officer's ditto.

"Their marriages are conducted without much trouble or annoyance to either party: the girls remain in an empty house, and the young men in the *Morang*, where after playing on the hollow trunk of a tree without singing, which I believe they never do, they all run into the house where the girls are, and each man takes his favorite: this is with the *lower orders* of course."

It is very probable that this is the case where parties may not have it in their power to offer a feast on the occasion. Were there not some such alternative, marriages would be less frequent than they now are. Mr. Robinson has obtained other information on this subject, and offers in his excellent work the following account of the ceremony:—

"Marriages among the Nagas are not contracted in childhood, as among the Hindoos, nor do the men generally marry young. This probably arises in a great measure from the difficulty of procuring the means of paying the parents of the bride the expected *douceur*, on giving the suitor their daughter to wife. Hence, the youth who wishes to espouse a girl, if accepted, agrees to serve her father for a term of years, generally limited to the period at which she may Mr. Robinson's opinion.

be considered marriageable. At the end of his servitude, a house is constructed for the young couple by their parents, who also supply them with a small stock of pigs, fowls, and rice. A long previous training has fully qualified the young bride to enter upon the duties of her new station, and the value of her services is generally so well appreciated, that nothing is more prompt than the vengeance of a Naga for any insult offered to his laborious partner; his spear gives the ready reply to any remark derogatory to her honor."

Celebration of births.

The occasion of a birth is celebrated with feasting and rioting. If it be a male child the party consists of men, and if a female, of women. In former times, tradition has it, that a child born before the natural period was strangled.

Methods of disposing of their dead.

Their methods of disposing of the dead in some measure resemble the modes adopted by the Australian savages. The body being first washed, is placed on a bamboo platform opposite the house of the deceased, and watched with care that flies or other insects may be kept off for a couple of days or more, when it is well covered with leaves, branches of trees, &c. Hidden to view whilst the work of decomposition progresses, the habitation is deserted for a time, but re-occupied on the cessation of any offensive odour. The skull, if it be of a man, has an apartment erected for it near the spot, in which, together with his daw and spear, made fast with a portion of hair from the heads of female relations, it is finally deposited. It is said that at times, on other ranges, the leaves are allowed to be removed by relatives, and that on every visit each gives the head of the corpse a twist so as to effect an early separation of the skull. Other accounts state, that, in some tribes, the corpse when laid on the platform goes through the process of desiccation, by a fire being lighted beneath, and carefully tended, until all the moisture has been gradually evaporated.

Feasts, songs, and dances follow.

At the conclusion of every ceremony, a feast is provided by the male relatives of the deceased, and is followed up with songs and dances, until (as they suppose) his spirit has quitted their village for ever, which departure is supposed to be about midnight. Female mortality seldom causes grief, unless in such an instance as the following, which the Reverend Mr Bronson, an American Missionary, has thus described:

The Revd. Mr. Bronson's description of the final disposal of a chief's wife.

" This day was the completion of the sixth month after the death of a wife of one of their chiefs. Their custom is to allow the corpse to remain six months in the house, at the expiration of which time the ceremonies I have this day witnessed must be performed. In the morning, two large buffaloes, several hogs, and a great number of fowls, were killed for the occasion. About noon, numbers of Nages from the neighbouring villages, dressed in a most fanciful manner, and equipped for battle, arrived. After beating several gongs of different sizes, so arranged as to form a sort of harmony with the music of drums, they marched to the house where the decaying corpse lay, each man bearing a shield, a spear, and a *daw*. They then commenced singing and dancing with such a regularity of step and voice as surprised me. They sang in the Abor tongue, and my interpreter informed me that all their songs are borrowed from the Abors, with whom they hold daily intercourse. I was allowed to attend in company with two of the chiefs, who interpreted to me the song, the substance of which is as follows:

" 'What divinity has taken away our friend? Who are you?—Where do you live? In heaven, on the earth, or under the earth? Who are you? Shew yourself. If we had known of your coming we would have speared you.'

" The above was first pronounced by the chorister. The whole company then answered it by exclaiming, 'Yes,' at the same time waving their huge glittering spears towards heaven in defiance of the evil spirit who was supposed to have occasioned the death. The chorister continues, 'We would have cut you in pieces, and eaten your flesh.' 'Yes,' responded the warriors, brandishing their daws, as if impatient for the battle. 'If you had apprised us of your coming, and asked our permission, we would have reverenced you; but you have secretly taken one of us, and now we will curse you.' 'Yes,' responded the warriors. This is the substance of what they sang, though varied and repeated many times; the noise of music and dancing continued nearly all night. During the greater part of the following day the same ceremonies were repeated. At the setting of the sun, a large company of young women came around the corpse, and completely covered it with leaves and flowers, after which it was carried to a small hill adjacent, and burnt amid the festivities of the people: thus closed this painful scene."

Theft is considered the most despicable of crimes—its punishment.

Of all crimes, they consider theft the greatest, and the punishment follows immediately on detection. The wrists and ancles, fastened with rattan, are brought together by an additional binding, and in this shape the detected is carried to the top of a high summit; and rolled down the side. Meeting in its fall, short stumps of trees, and other temporary checks, the body is generally torn to pieces, before reaching the bottom.

Appearance of a comet, and the alarm it occasions amongst them.

The appearance of a comet spreads alarm and despair around: during its presence, the Nagas abstain from their usual levity, and feastings, and some from even the actual necessaries of life. It is not uncommon amongst them to go into the forests during its exhibition, and remain there until report reaches them of its disappearance. The last one was supposed to be the prognosticator of a cessation of the Company's government over the plains of Assam—it indicating, in their opinion, the approach of the *Mauns* or

Burmese from the eastward, who on their march were, in overwhelming forces, to cut up their tribes, and fire every village within their reach. On this occasion these hardy mountaineers certainly evinced a degree of cowardice, which former boastings, and certainly chivalric qualifications, would not have induced one to expect that they were capable of displaying.

Some do not possess permanent abodes but migrate at auspicious periods.

Some amongst them have no settled place of residence, but like the *Meerees*, and others on this frontier, migrate after a certain period's stay, from one hill to another. When this is the case, the whole village moves together, men, women, children, hogs, buffaloes, and oxen, the former bearing their children, stock, and other domestic appurtenances—nothing but the habitations remain, amongst which vegetation rapidly rises, and in the course of a year or two its remains, and the paths around it are closed, encumbered with jungle.

Removal from one spot to another.

On the unanimous selection of a new spot, they halt and settle, and clear away for the first night or two, a portion of the forest which they appropriate to their women and cattle, surrounded by spears. Such a scene is very romantic, and reminds one in some degree of a gipsy camp. Their conversation on the occurrence is replete with fun and good humour, varied by singing and shouts of laughter all the night. On these occasions, it is not an unfrequent occurrence for them to lose one or more of their party by tigers—and it is to prevent such losses that they remain awake until the dawn. As soon as a clearance has been effected they erect their dwelling places, and with an incredible degree of quickness a village is formed. Their motives for removing every five or six years is believed to be on account of supposed exhaustion of soil, from the repeated gathering of crops, and the process of manuring is not esteemed by them a profitable one, although for such purposes they are plentifully supplied with means.

Existence of coal on the Naga ranges.

Coal (*van hi*) has been found imbedded in parts of these hills, but difficulty of transit is a serious drawback to the working of it. The Nagas convert it into no use whatever—but have an idea that it is a vegetable decomposition. Along the whole line of these mountains, this mineral has been found to exist, cropping out here and there—and shewing coal of no inferior quality.

On the Noa-dehing, and its affluent, the Dupha Pannee.

" In tracing its appearance from the most easterly or remote site of Upper Assam, the first to notice is the coal found on the Noa-dehing and its affluent the Dupha Pannee, in the hilly country, to the south and east of the Bramahkhund. The site of this bed is too remote for it to be of any practical benefit under existing circumstances, as it is beyond the reach of being profitably worked, and introduced to the navigable part of the Bramahpootra.

In the bed of the Manirup river.

" The next vein of coal to be noticed is that discovered in the bed of the Manirup river, a small stream that empties itself into the Boree-dehing. The coal is considerably free from earthy or slaty matter, and exhibits frequently ligneous fibre, though like the last it is in too remote a situation to be easily available for useful purposes."

On the Tippum hills.

On the *Tippum* hills, the lower set of the Naga ranges, coal is very plentiful; and this spot possesses many advantages over the other measures that have been discovered, on account both of its proximity to water carriage, and ready command of labour.

At Teroo and on the Bheeta Namsangeea ranges.

On a hill to the eastward of Borhat, it again makes its appearance at *Terroo,* on the Suffry stream—and on the *Bheeta Namsangeea* ranges, where it was worked by a Mr. A. H. Landers, Special Assistant to the Commissioner, in 1841-42.

Opinion of the Coal Committee on it.

The Coal Committee have reported favorably on it; but it is to be regretted that numerous natural impediments, present themselves to its easier transmission; so many indeed, that it is to be feared no practical benefit will ever be derived from the working of them. Its mean specific gravity has been ascertained to be about 1.288, containing,

Mean volatile and other matter,	45.4
Carbon,..............................	50.4
Ash, ...	4.2
	100.

Among other mineralogical resources of this chain may be mentioned Petroleum springs, exuding a sort of asphaltum; slate, peat, brine springs, yielding about one-sixth of their weight in common salt.—Iron, (*ján*) in a considerable quantity, which is found embedded in a crust of red sandstone, composed of quartz, felspar and mica. It is smelted by the Nagas and turned into use; but although their furnaces are not the most perfect yet they reduce the ore with facility and economy.—Limestone, but not sufficiently clammy to indicate its importance, nor, indeed, possessing a proportionate quantity of lime to render it worth burning. **Other mineralogical resources.**

Gold (*Kam*) is washed down from these hills into the streams in the plains, but its original resting-places have never been discovered. In Assam the sands are washed for the acquirement of it in the cold weather, when the rivers are at a low ebb, generally about the junction of one of them with the Bramahpootra. It is not supposed that the *Sonwals*, or washers ever realize any thing very considerable, on the contrary it sometimes is loss of time to them. Particulars of the process are registered by Muneeram Sheristadar, per Captain Hannay, in a journal of the Asiatic Society, Vol. 7, part 2. As these particles of gold must be washed from the Naga ranges, this subject bas been introduced that future travellers may bestow careful attention on it. **Gold.**

Earthquakes are numerous, and perhaps a **Earthquakes.**

cause, however imperceptible, of the extraordinary features of these hills by gradual elevation and depression. Sometimes they are experienced for two and three days together, at certain intervals, the shock passing usually from north to south. How they may be influenced by volcanic sources here, or if by any local electric phenomena, is a subject for scientific enquiry. They are preceded by a close sultriness of atmosphere, and are often so severe as to raze habitations. The Nagas are much afraid of them, and they confidently attribute their presence to a failure of sufficient adoration.

Bridges of rude construction.

Their bridges (*síks*) over the mountain torrents are rude, but still secure, and to the stranger appear singularly strange. At the formidable height of fifty and sixty feet from the surface of the waters, connectors, made of strong rattan, are passed across, stretched, and fastened on either slope to some secure tree or rock. Another one, a little higher above this set, serves (to use a nautical phrase,) as a life-line, and encircling both these is a ring of three or four feet in diameter, made from creepers; to this is attached a long rattan on each side for the purpose of hauling a traveller over, which is effected by his keeping his head and legs in a sitting posture on one side of it, counteracted by a peculiar position of the arms on the other. When the hauling lines may by accident have dropped in the stream, or where there may be no one to drag over on the opposite side, one of the most nimble is selected to cross first, secure them, and otherwise assist on the other side—not in all cases a very enviable task.

Paths.

Their paths (*lam's*) to a traveller are equally perplexing, though unaccompanied with danger, and so intricate are they, that it is often with difficulty that one can manage to keep in his right track. They appear to think this labyrinthical confusion more conducive to their safety, by the improbability of other tribes attempting to attack, where access to the place is not thoroughly known. If during a tempest any trees should fall over and block up an old pass, they will cut *round* it, each in his turn, as they march one by one clearing away rattan and other jungle. This fact will give an idea, from the continual falling of trees, how harassing these pathways are to a stranger; and new ones continually appearing, how disagreeable to travel on even with shoes, for it is seldom in making the clearance that they cut shrub or creeper at the bottom of the plant; three or four inches of pointed stump is invariably left from the cutting up and down, with their *daws*. Elephants, that have been up on service suffered severely in the feet, and no sensible man who had any regard for his animal would use it on these hills more than he could possibly help.

A new fruit.

A delicious acid fruit, with a leechee kind of flesh, is peculiar to these ranges. Some of the seeds, leaves, fruit, and suckers, have been sent to the Agricultural Society's garden at Gohatti.

Sissoo seeds. *Sissoo* seeds were given them through the kind attention of the Commissioner, but they could not be persuaded to apply them to any use.

Wild coffee. Wild coffee is found on many of the hills, but bear few and insignificant berries.

Cotton. Cotton (*co-pàh*) is cultivated by them to a small extent: the Commissioner sent up a large quantity of this also for distribution. It was duly and equally portioned out to them, but they did not admire the staple so much as their own, although this was the finest Georgian and Sea Island seed. For separating, and clearing it, they use a *Churka*, somewhat similar to the Assamese one. They appropriate the article to no use, but take it down to the plains for barter.

Potatoes. The author once gave them a maund of potatoes for planting, but naturally enough they appropriated them to a different purpose, and afterwards to the question "how they were thriving?" received a reply, "that they were better than their own yam, and would be glad of another supply."

Agriculture not extensive. Agriculture being carried on only to a certain extent, they prefer their own primitive method to any others that are suggested to them. The partial revival of it, now in effect amongst the Assamees, may years hence possibly induce them to a change, but at present it is difficult to remove their jealous impression. The growth, or use, (with the exception of the chillie and some ginger,) of those vegetables which constitute the excellence of a good currie, is unknown to them, but the writer once prevailed on one of the chiefs, in order that cultivation of them might be practised, to taste a table currie, but he has no reason to suppose that this effort led to any results.

With peppers particularly.

The cultivation of the poppy is but small, and they depend for their supplies on the plains. When they do manufacture it, it is in a manner similar to the Assamese method, an account of which will be found at the end of this book.

Poppy.

Of hemp, an article cultivated nearly all over the world, they are totally ignorant, both of its narcotic properties, and the use of its fibres. The latter is not, however, extraordinary, as they are neither fishermen nor boatmen, and in Assam it is principally used by the *Doms* or fishermen. Of the use of *cocoons* they are equally ignorant.

Hemp, and cocoons.

They indulge largely in tobacco, which they chew with *pàn*, *tamul*, and portions of aromatic barks indigenous to their hills. It is cultivated by them in small quantities, but not to an extent proportionate to their wants.

Tobacco.

An Alpine strawberry is frequently met with on the slopes of cleared hills, and generally near streams. It bears a very pretty little red fruit,

Species of Alpine strawberry.

with a corresponding-sized leaf, but is destitute of taste: appearing in clusters when ripe, the spots on which they grow enhance considerably the pleasing appearance of the villages.

Sorrels. *Sorrel*, of different kinds, occurs in all parte of the forests. The species most esteemed is a large-leaved one with a red prickly stem. The Nagas are very fond of it, and on marching between streams of water, often stop to search for it, with a view to check their thirst. It is very acid and juicy.

Kind of potatoe. By digging towards the root of a certain parasite, most generally in low spots, an esculent vegetable is found assimilating in nearly every respect to the long red potatoe, brought to the English markets, and which, partakes when cooked of the same mealy flavor; these are much sought after by them, together with the *Kutchoo* or wild kind of yam.

Cardamoms. Cardamoms are known to exist, but are not procurable in large quantities. In appearance they more nearly resemble those of Malabar, than the produce of Patna. The plant, as with every thing else that they find to be valuable to us, they are now so jealous of, that a plant can scarcely be got from them.

Cassia. Cassia, or *Tez-pat* of the market, is indigenous to the hills, but has not been found in sufficient quantity to warrant the belief of its ever becoming an article of trade, without cultivation and extension.

Cloves are said to exist in the Abor ranges, but no opportunity has hitherto been afforded to the European, for authentic testimony, although assurance of the fact has been offered on shewing them some real ones, and that it was by no means an uncommon plant. On removing the dried flower-bud, which forms the head of the clove, from the stem, on one occasion, it was again produced; but they detected the fraud, and unhesitatingly repeated the fact of its existence. **Cloves.**

The writer never had sufficient leisure at command to follow up enquiries on this subject; but confesses his doubts as to what they imagine to be the real clove, although they reported the appearance of the tree, and leaf correctly.

A fruit was also once brought in from the Abor ranges resembling in every appearance the *nutmeg*—even to the mace that surrounded it. It had not fully ripened, and was held within its pod. An imprudent show of delight at the discovery, confirmed their suspicion of its value, and other seeds were at once withheld. Had but a practical botanist been on the spot, considerable anxiety might have been spared, although it is probable that gathering the fruit would still have been prohibited. A gentleman highly qualified for the task, Mr. Masters, is now actively engaged in researches on these very hills, and it is yet possible that this nutmeg may be shewn to him. It has been argued that the plant affects the neigh- **Nutmeg: probability of its existence on these ranges.**

bourhood of the sea—and those habitats only where the soil is impregnated with salt. But is it not possible that, from the scores of brine-springs on these hills, it may be cherished equally here, as on the sea side? Influenced by a saline atmosphere, it is not; nevertheless, the acknowledged fact of its requiring this kind of habitat, leads to the suspicion of its presence on the neighbouring ranges.

Gums and varnishes.

The choice gums and varnishes which exude from many of the trees in these forests, could they be collected in sufficient quantities, would command in our English markets a ready sale. That, from the *Mackoi* (a species of *Dipterocarpus*) in forcing its way from between the crevices of the bark, is perfectly colourless, resembling in appearance a clear icicle. That from the *Nahore*, (*Mœsua ferrea*,) so classed by Mr. Masters,* has an aromatic odour, and differs in appearance from the *Mackoi* gum, being of a light amber colour, and not compact as is the case with the former. These two trees are in every sense remarkable. The *Mackoi* often grows to the height of a hundred and fifty feet, rising as straight as a ship's mast, without a single lateral branch as an impediment to its beauty, and at the root the writer has seen them *seven* and *eight* feet in diameter, a slice

* The blossoms of Mœsua ferrea are to be found in every bazar in a dried state, under the name of *Nagkesun*, being used in medicine as well as esteemed for their fragrance. —LINDLEY'S NAT. SYS. p. 75.

from which, would make a most magnificent table in one piece. Firm, durable, and close-grained, it is worthy of particular notice. The *Nahore* in its power of resistance to the axe, again supercedes the *Mackoi;* so notoriously hard is it that a dozen axes may be shivered to pieces, before the tree will fall. It produces a fruit somewhat resembling the chesnut, of an unctuous nature ; from which a beautiful oil can be expressed having the same odour as the gum. At night its delightful fumes, when burnt, render the article quite a luxury. Virtues of the Nahore and Mackoi trees.

The *Oolung* is also a remarkably straight tree, but not of so good a grain as the *Mackoi.* No gum is obtainable from it, but it serves capitally for purposes of building. Oolung.

The *Ficus elastica,* from which excellent caoutchouc can be prepared, is conspicuous for the elasticity which is characteristic of the article. Ficus elastica.

The *Thea viridis,* or tea tree, in the Naga hills, produces much smaller leaves than the plants of Assam, and the produce is in consequence much finer, and better adapted for sale. Tea tree.

The *Seelaw* (Naga name). From the bark of this tree when well beaten, long fibres are obtained, with which are manufactured rude cloths, ropes, &c. Seelaw.

The *Jeeloo* (Naga name.) The stem of this when scooped out, forms an instrumental appen- Jeeloo.

dage to their *Morang*, as will hereafter be described.

Oranges. Their oranges (*Mú-thúlá*) are of a good *sort.* They are of two kinds; the one sweet, like Mandarin fruit, and the other larger, with a slight acidity in it. The men seldom eat them, regarding either kind, as a food for only women, and children, who freely partake of them.

Jack. Jack, the *Kathāl*, are abundant in the villages, but no particular value is attached to them.

Oak. There is a species of oak, (*Hingoree,*) which produces an acorn, but the wood is of inferior quality.

Sterculia urens. The bark of the *Sterculia urens* (Roxb.) is occasionally brought into use, being converted into ropes, which often form parts of suspension-bridges. " The bark is of a light color and very smooth; its outer coat is thin, transparent, covered with a farinaceous substance, and peels off like the exterior pellicle of the birch bark; inwardly it is fibrous and netted."

Pàn. The *Pàn* leaf is mostly supplied to the Assamese from these hills; they have two kinds, called by them the *akham niàp* or hot leaf, and the *ki-no-o-niàp* or smelling leaf. It is raised from slips, and in its growth attached to forest trees.

Myrica integrifolia. The *Myrica integrifolia,* (Roxb.) or *Nagatenga,* bears an acid fruit which is much enjoyed by the Nagas.

The useful *Bamboo* is found in great abundance, in groves on the tops of hills, on their slopes, and in the ravines; its stems are appropriated to the purposes of building, also for ornaments, cooking pots, furniture, and spear-shafts; and its leaves, shoots, and seed, often form an article of food. **Bamboo.**

The most valuable kind is what is commonly called *Janti bàngh;* it grows to a very *good* size, and for building is esteemed indispensable.

Deo bàngh—this is a smaller species, supposed to be common in China, and is used for spear-shafts, baskets, and personal ornaments. It is more common amongst the tribes to the eastward than on these particular hills.

Kako bàngh—very common over all the ranges, but not much sought for, or in fact ever used, except in the absence of the *Janti bàngh*, the stems being crooked and liable to early decay.

The *rattan* is equally useful to the Naga—it is found in all parts of the forest, of different varieties. **Rattan.**

The *A-chan rí* is preferred for uniting bamboos or timbers, where strength and durability may be a primary object.

The rind of the *Naga rí* is generally converted into ornaments, and occasionally the plant may be found in lengths of eighty or a hundred feet.

The *Nagonee rí* is held in little estimation.

Cocos.

Among the palms, a species of *Cocos*, (Linn.) is found on the left banks of the Boree Deehing, or north boundary of these hills. This genus has been supposed to court the sea side *only*. It bears fruit in clusters, each seed about the size of a common marble, though oval; and is attached to the soil on which it rests merely by a collection of innumerable short black fibres.

Brine springs.

There are several brine springs on these hills from which salt is manufactured by evaporation, and the process being rather a novel one, an account of it here, may interest those who have had few opportunities of learning the practices and customs of these strange races.

Their primitive system of manufacture, and barter, has not been improved, or altered, by European agency.

As in all uncivilized nations, the inhabitants are averse to adopt any new system of manufacture introduced by foreigners, however much such new system might be productive of good to themselves—so is it in this instance; for more than one party has made every effort to convince them that their present mode of manufacture is an erroneous one, compared with the better plan of using iron vessels. They are entirely dependent on this article for their livelihood, and when prepared, they carry it down to the plains of Assam, and barter it for rice and opium. A thorough satisfaction of interchange, I have always remarked; and as they evince no wish to try any new experiments, either in manufacture or mode of disposal, no strenuous effort has been made by the officers of Government to compel it.

Including a few wells in the Pannee Dwariah chief's possessions, no less than eighty-five have been ascertained to exist, either producing, or which may be made to produce, salt. Our Government are supposed to have an interest in four of the Namsang wells; three undoubtedly belong to it entirely, and in the other we have a claim of eight per cent., or eight *hals* out of the hundred. The right of British Government to shares in some wells.

In the Bor Dwariah possessions, the Government is entitled to work two, out of seventeen *hals* in one well, during the night, and two out of twenty-seven, during the day time, in another. In the Bor Dwariah possessions.

The Panee Dwariahs are not so fortunate in their natural productions, particularly in brine springs; and an interest in one well is all that the Company lay claim to, from which they work one *hal* out of twenty during the night. In the Panee Dwariah possessions.

The positions of these wells are perhaps remarkable, being always found in the beds of rapids, and hence they are only available for salt manufacture in the cold season, or in the absence of inundation. Position of them.

It is not unusual for the Assam Pikes to go up to the hills and manufacture the article for themselves: when this is the case, they invariably carry up, for satisfaction to the Naga proprietor, some rice, fowls, tamul, &c., and pay to the chieftain a proportionate quantity of their produce which they realize. The pikes themselves often manufacture.

Size of springs, &c. &c.

The wells being natural, vary in size, some being very deep, and producing more or less brine, averaging from two and a half, to three feet in diameter, and the shaft is not unfrequently protected by a lining of wood or a hollow tree; a common bamboo *chungah* does duty as a bucket, when attached to a stick or piece of rattan.

Place of manufacture.

The place of manufacture is generally selected at a convenient distance between jungle and the well, so that fuel should be near at hand for

Description of a hal.

feeding the furnace. The *hal* is of mud work, sometimes sixteen or eighteen feet long, and from three to four broad; perhaps three feet in height, with sufficient space all up the centre to form a flue, and admit these *chungahs* or joints of bamboo to rest on it. The *hal*, in some instances, is covered with a grass thatch, and has an adjoining hut elevated on poles, used as a sleeping place for those parties who come to manufacture—the elevation of such a domicile being evidently necessary on account of the forests

Process of manufacture.

abounding in wild animals of all descriptions. The fire being lighted at one end, the *chungahs* are placed close together on the top, at right angles to the building, and are filled and constantly replenished with brine as evaporation takes place. Con-

Adulteration.

siderable imposition is now being practised, which was not formerly the case, and which will, in all probability, as these tribes advance in civilization, by introducing impurities into the article, such as ashes or sand, which, when offered for sale, tells of itself in weight. This must necessarily be the upper surface of the article, the salt, which is of the most delicate white colour, having settled at the bottom; it is supposed to contain a large proportion of saltpetre, and for domestic purposes, it is objected to. The Professor of Chemistry here has received specimens for analysis, and it might be desirable to enquire into its properties.

Chemical properties.

Policy of retention.

Considered in a political point of view, it would appear highly necessary for Government to have retained both their own, as well as their interest in other wells, as affording the means of keeping up a communication, and preserving (as neighbours) tranquillity amongst them. Such was done until an attack from the tribes eastward of them induced the chieftains to claim protection from us, which was promised on their binding themselves over to refer all disputes to a British court for arbitration. The Commissioner of the province has, since then, made over to them not only the wells, but has ceased enforcing a duty which had hitherto been levied on all salt sold in the plains, a custom which had for many years prevailed, and was, in the first instance, demanded by one of the Assamese Rajahs.

Total List of the Wells, as registered by Mr. C. R. Strong, Sub-Assistant Commissioner.

Nam-Sang Wells.

Names of the wells.

No. 1 Somchee.
2 Deare Mahong.
3 Tangjung, (shut.)
4 Lang Mah.
5 Long Kah.
6 Nol Mahong.
7 Dagullee.
8 Tanga Baka.
9 Bomarah.
10 Boogallee, (shut.)
11 Chorie Pat, (do.)
12 Bor Low, (do.)
13 Sonoo, (do.)
14 Neenattie, (do.)
15 Phokalla, Namsang Koonbow's Well.
16 Oreegooree.
17 Now Mohong.
18 Sogie.
19 Boolooka Gooree.
20 Mooree.
21 Seel Koobollee.
22 Boulee, (shut.)
23 Bochoroo.
24 Thakoroo.
25 Bowman.
26 Thang Sa.
27 Dou Pang.
28 Hooroo Lang Pete, (1 hal.)

No. 29 Bor Long Petee, (1 hal.) Names of the wells.

30 Boogoorie Gooree, (shut.)

31 Roodallee.

32 Doosorah Seil Kooliale.

33 Jooree, (shut.)

34 Neon Mohong.

35 Lakoo Mohong.

36 Nolla Mohong.

37 Degulleelang.

38 Oper Chune Putton, (shut.)

39 Namchurn, (do.)

40 Karree.

41 Molleecha.

42 Non Mohong, (shut.)

43 Bon Pollo.

44 Kapeelee.

45 Bangooree.

46 Nonjon Tingal.

47 Boul Mohong.

48 Bakullee.

49 Bonder Dom.

50 Morannee Morra.

51 Don Domar Tingal Sobang.

52 Jakoorah Mohong.

53 Chomaie.

54 Jepam.

Bor Dwar Wells.

No. 1 Nam Ton.

2 Kasowa.

3 Don Mohong.

4 Galo Gooree.

Names of the wells.

No. 5 Kampie.
6 Roopie.
7 Sorah Laug Pete Mohong.
8 Bogiernie.
9 Bhal.
10 Naringa.
11 Bangie.
12 Karrie.
13 Bougooree.
14 Banguriph.
15 Doosoorah Bhot Maugh.
16 Lallee Katoree.
17 Chie.
18 Bor Mohong.
19 Doosoora Sirra.

Pannee Dwar Wells.

No. 1 Katal Gooree.
2 Gola Galee.
3 Ramcha, (1 Haut Sirkarree.)
4 Bowpilling.
5 Tersara Copeelee.
6 Doosoorah Diepang.
7 Mooree.
8 Lam Mohong.
9 Bakee.
10 Sooncha.
11 Rahadie.
12 Takoo Well.

There is also a closed well near Jaipur. Each man that traded in this article formerly, in addition to Naga fees, was compelled to pay to the

Assamese government, monthly, half a maund of salt,—to the *Hautquah* eight seers, to the *Kagottee* or writer two seers, and to the *Bundahree*, or godown-keeper, one.

Healthiness of the hills.

Of the salubrity of these hills generally, people now begin to form very favorable notions, as compared with Assam. The mortality is not so great with the Nagas as with the Assamese, although in one sense this is easily accounted for, their industry contrasting so much with the indolence of the Assamese. The incessant privations which they endure, sometimes, during the rains, depending entirely on the forest for food when cut off by torrents from the plains, their constant action either in ascending or descending the sides of steep mountains, and the much less quantity of opium that is consumed by them, naturally accounts for their mostly athletic and healthy appearance.

Tea soils.

The soil of those portions of the Naga hills on which the tea tree is found, contains, in 200 parts,—

Water,...	37
Fresh fibre,	1
Vegetable matter,	$5\frac{1}{2}$
Silex,	135
Alumina,	11
Oxide of Iron,	$4\frac{1}{3}$

China and Assam tea districts.

The largest tea districts in China are found between the parallels of 27 and 31 degrees of north latitude, whilst in Assam and its adjoining hills it embraces a district of nearly a degree and a half, or between 26° 15' and 27° 36.' Mr. Cunningham, an able botanist who has travelled amongst the China mountains, states that the plant delights *in summitalibus montium*, although neither this gentleman nor Dr. Abel had ever attempted to reach the *highest* points of its cultivation. Messrs. Gordon and Gutzlaff, also, on their visit to the *Ankoy* tea hills, found the plant growing luxuriantly on the "tops and sides of mountains."

Tea found in a variety of soils. From the great extent of territory over which, and from the variety of situations in which tea is produced, there can be little doubt that it is grown in a variety of soils, though there are no doubt certain physical conditions which are best suited to the production of the *finest flavoured* teas. The plantations which Dr. Abel saw were in a kind of gravelly soil, formed either of disintegrated sandstone, or primary rocks.

Note by Major Jenkins. Captain Jenkins, Agent to the Governor General on the north-east frontier, in reply to a circular of the 3d March 1834, on the subject of tea localities, mentions that—"The part directly under us ranges from six thousand to eight thousand feet, and that, further east, the mountain attains a height of ten thousand feet, and the valleys and beds of streams are from two thousand five hundred to four thousand feet above the sea."

Judging from reports of scientific gentlemen

on this subject, and comparing localities with those of China, these Naga hills must undoubtedly bear better sorts of tea than is found in the plains of Assam. One of the Calcutta Journals about three years ago, on manufactured specimens being submitted to a judge of the article observes— Comparison of localities.

"We have just had some tea of gunpowder quality shewn to us, the produce of Hookon Juri one of the Naga hills, and consequently the first tea manufactured north-eastward of Assam. The specimen has a strong high flavor and a remarkable aroma, which will, there is no doubt, prove a strong recommendation to it in the home market, where also, being capable of landing at a cheap rate, it will come in serviceably to revive and strengthen the China article, and give the poorer classes especially a strong wholesome beverage within their means of obtaining." Extract from a Calcutta Journal.

"The prevailing characters of the soil are lightness and porousness: its prevailing color is yellow or reddish yellow, which generally becomes more developed as the depth increases, up to a certain point when it passes into sand." Characters of tea soil.

The leaves are gathered from one to four times during the year, according to the age of the tree. Most commonly there are three periods of gathering commencing in April. Gathering of leaves.

The measures which have now been in progress for the cultivation of the plant and the Hopes of ultimate success.

manufacture of tea, lead eventually to the anticipation of very favorable results, and the immense wealth which has flowed for a century and a half from Great Britain and her colonies to a foreign country will, it is hoped, henceforth be distributed amongst British subjects, and a new source of lucrative employment opened up to thousands.

Partiality of the Nagas to the beverage.

The Nagas are beginning to look on tea, manufactured according to Chinese style, as a grateful beverage; notwithstanding they still entertain the impression that our wandering over their forests in search of the plant is a mere pretext to see their country, and if found to be plentifully supplied with valuable productions that appropriation will follow. The idea may be indulged, that years hence both Assamees and hill-rangers will leave off the use of opium and other intoxicating drugs for the better substitute of an indigenous, and easily manufactured article.

Average produce of plants.

The average produce of a single plant has not even yet been satisfactorily proved in its different stages of growth, and it would, under the circumstances, be premature to offer an opinion of its capabilities.

Mr. Robinson's correspondent on the subject is evidently qualified to report on the shrub, and the writer thinks he cannot do better than extract from that gentleman's work a description of it—

" The ordinary height of the shrub is from five

to eight feet, though it occasionally attains a far greater size.* It is a polyandrous plant of the natural order of *Ternstiomicæ*. The flowers which open early in spring appear upon the plant about a month, are smaller in size and much less elegant than those that render some species of the Cammellia so attractive. They are about an inch in diameter, slightly odorous, and of a pure white colour. They proceed from the axils of the branches, and stand on short foot-stalks, at the most two or three together, but usually solitary. There are five or six imbricate sepals or leaves supporting the blossom, which fall off after the flower has expanded, and leave from six to nine petals surrounding a great number of yellow stamens that are joined together in such a manner at their bases, as to form a sort of floral coronal. The seeds are enclosed in a smooth hard capsule, of a flattish triangular shape, which is interiorly divided into two, three, and even five cells—each containing a firm, white, and somewhat oily nut about the size of a hazel-nut, of a bitterish and nauseous taste. They ripen in December and January,† the stem is generally bushy, with numerous branches bearing a very dense foliage and in its general appearance is not unlike a myrtle, though not so symmetrical as

Description of the shrub.

---

* The writer has seen them, with all due respect to Mr. R., nearly 60 feet in height, and the stem two cubits and a half in circumference—*in its wild state.*

† October and November on the Naga hills.

that plant. The wood is light-colored, close-grained, of great comparative density, and when freshly cut or peeled gives off a strong smell resembling that of the black currant bush. The leaves are alternate, on short, thick, channelled foot-stalks, coriaceous, or leathery, but smooth and shining, of a dark green colour, and a longish elliptic form, with a blunt notched point, and serrated, except at the base. It is needless to mention that these leaves are the valuable part of the plant. They are, however, a good deal affected by the site in which the plant is grown, whether under the thick umbrage of large trees, or in open spots exposed to the influence of the sun's rays, as well as by the nature of the soil in which the plant is found.

Tea used by the Singphoes.

Tea has hitherto been the favourite beverage of those hill tribes in whose vicinity the wild plant has been found. The Singphoes have long known and drank the tea, but their mode of preparing it is very different from ours. The young and tender leaves are first plucked and dried in the sun; by some they are exposed alternately to the night dews and the heat of the sun for three successive days, whilst by others they are put into flat hot pans and turned about till quite dry. This done, the leaves are placed in the hollow of a bamboo and driven firmly down by means of a stick—the bamboo being at the same time held in the heat of a fire. When full, the ends of the bamboo are tied up with leaves, and then hung

Mode of preparation.

up in places where they may be exposed to the smoke of the fire. Thus prepared, the tea is said to keep good for years.

Another method.

In other places the natives have a different mode of manufacture. Holes are dug in the earth, the sides of which are lined with large leaves. The tea is then boiled, the decoction thrown away, and the leaves themselves are buried in the earth. This is done with the view of reducing the leaves to a state of fermentation; and when this has been effected, the leaves are put into hollow bamboos, and thus prepared are taken to market. When intended for use, the leaves are boiled, and the infusion is drank.

Butia preparation.

The Butias are said to be particularly attached to this beverage. Their supplies are, however, imported overland from Pekin. The liquor they drink is extremely unlike what we are used to under the same name. It is a compound of water, flour, butter, salt, and bohea tea, with some other astringent ingredients, all boiled, beat up, and intimately blended together.

Anticipation of successful results from the cultivation of the plant.

From the well known fact of tea being the favorite drink of those tribes in whose vicinity it has been found, as well as from the immense quantity expended in the adjacent kingdom of Butan, it would appear far from chimerical to anticipate a very successful result from the general culture of the plant in Assam, were it merely with the view of rendering it a staple article of trade with the regions in which it is so extensively consumed; and where, from the peculiar mode of preparing it for use, less skill in its culture would be necessary than in those varieties intended for European markets.

Consumption of tea in Teshu Lumbu.

Captain Turner estimated that the value of the tea consumed in the district of Teshu Lumbu alone amounted to *seven lakhs of rupees* per annum; and considering that it is imported from Pekin by a land journey of eight months' duration, and then comparing the regions it is compelled to traverse, with the nature of the country that intervenes between Assam and Butan, and the time that caravans would respectively take, in reaching the same place from Pekin and Gohatti, it would seem very probable that were the tea trade carried on with Butan alone it would tend in no small measure to promote the future welfare of the country.

Probability of all these hill tribes becoming good agriculturists.

One of the most favorable features in our tea prospects is the altered temper of our Singphoe "and Naga" subjects. Since the rule of the British government has been fairly established over the Muttuck country, and those intrigues put an end to, which, originating in the mistaken policy and jealousy of the Bar Senapati and his numerous sons, kept the whole frontier in perpetual disturbance, the Singphoe chiefs, always disunited amongst themselves, and willing to engage in any rencounter where there was a prospect of plunder, have either seen that the factions promoted by the chiefs of Muttuck were fomented for their own sinister purposes, or they have felt the necessity of submitting to a power which has now so nearly approached to them, and whose strength they clearly perceive they cannot resist. They have in consequence shewn an inclination to abandon their old habits of lawlessness and rapine, and turn their attention to agriculture, now become necessary for their subsistence.

Right of discovery.

The right of the discovery of the tea-plant has been a subject of much discussion : Captain Charlton doubtless deserves the credit.

The following account of the manufacture was drawn up for the use of the Agri-Horticultural Society of India :

" *Memorandum on the Manufacture, &c. of Black Tea, as practised in the Naga hills.*

" With reference to the recommendation of Mr. Charles Terry in his report on Mr. Sconce's sample of Chittagong tea, (published in the ninth number of the Society's Journal,) to the effect that it would be desirable that parties interested in the cultivation of this plant at Chittagong should have some particular account of the process adopted by the Tea Company, I have the pleasure, with a view to assist in carrying out this recommendation, to submit the accompanying notes, in the hope that the hints contained therein may prove acceptable to the Society, and useful to tea cultivators in general.

Picking season.

" I have for the last three seasons commenced picking my leaves from the 1st to the 8th and

9th of April, and I should be disposed to think that this might be done in most factories where a few days rain had fallen towards the end of March, followed up by a hot sun, for I have found in some plantations where the forest has been only partially cleared, and the shrubs consequently protected from the sun, that the young leaves come out very languidly, and are necessarily more thick and brittle, than in those gardens where the plants are more exposed. Night dews are very acceptable during the manufacturing season, and by most planters are much courted.

Localities.

"The best localities for *sown* plantations is undoubtedly on the slopes of hills, without reference to magnetic directions, or on irregular undulating lands. Spots of indigenous tea have been found on the plains, but the plants do not thrive so well.

Light and room necessary in a tea house.

"In manufacturing I would recommend great care to be bestowed on the *building* of the tea house, (a sketch of a proper one accompanies this.) *Light* is indispensably necessary for watching the growing and fading colours of the teas, while being fired. *Room* for working is equally desirable, that your men may play freely, as quickness is so requisite in some parts of the process, that its absence is frequently the means of spoiling whole baskets full of the raw produce.

"Though windows in the day time are so much wanted, yet, good shutters for keeping out

Elevation
Scale 10 feet 1 Inch.

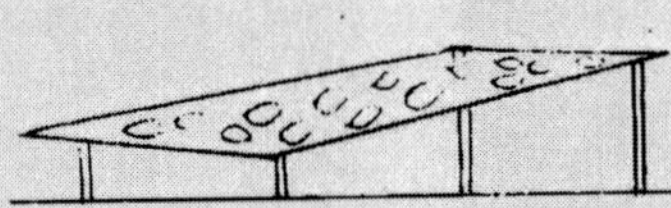

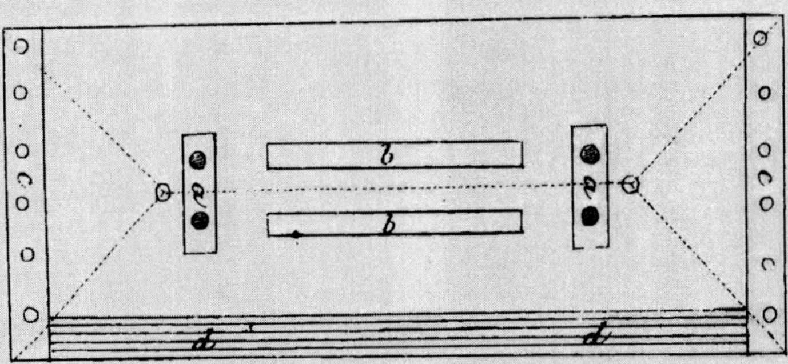

Ground Plan.

References.

a.a.	Tea pans.
b.b.	Rolling tables.
c.c.	Choolas.
d. d.	Dollah Racks.

the damp night air from the teas must be had, or it may be necessary to give them another firing, which any thing but improves the quality.

"In large factories, discipline, to command economy, is a grand thing to be attended to. Disci-pline.

"When each artizan has his own particular station in the teahouse, and is not allowed to move from it either to assist another, or leave the place altogether, it is astonishing what a quantity of extra work may be accomplished, and in the first and second crops it often happens that the young leaves grow so fast that many of the manufacturers are required out to assist in the plantations by day, leaving work in the tea house till mid-night. This system I should be inclined to deprecate, however, where it is *not actually necessary*, and only to save the leaves from entire loss, as the smoke from the different lamps required to light up the place must, however imperceptible when new, throw a foreign flavor, deteriorating from the aroma of such a delicate leaf as the tea. Particular stations for artizans. Smoke affects the tea.

"I need hardly observe that *cleanliness* should be carefully attended to by the planter both in his rolling tables and the hands of the artizans; for not having possibly any sensible effect on the leaves, still every delicately-minded man would wish others to eat or drink as pure an article as himself, and it is difficult to impress on the minds of natives the necessity of those frequent ablu- Cleanliness.

tions which are called for before commencing this operation.

Care in making implements for manufacture. "In a certain part of the process the leaves are rolled on large bamboo mat baskets, about three feet in diameter, with a rim of two or three inches all round it. The strictest attention should be paid to the making of these baskets, so that in the motion of rolling the leaves on it, they would not be *cut* by the harsh edges of the bamboo which is very often the case, as may be observed by any person on saturating a few leaves of any kind of black tea. These baskets should also be well seasoned before use by keeping them six or seven days under water, otherwise the planter is as liable to injure the *aroma* as well as the *appearance* of his tea.

Charcoal. "The *charcoal* used should be of the finest description; and requires almost as much care in selection, as the tea leaves themselves. I would myself recommend close-grained woods destitute of gum, and this should be burned under ground, in the Chinese manner; the moment a piece of charcoal is detected *smoking*, it should be removed, otherwise, the tea over it will be spoiled.

Rolling. "The process of *rolling* is perhaps the most difficult to learn, and it requires daily practice of some months to acquire a proper habit of it. It is effected by taking as many loose leaves from the tray or basket as can conveniently be compressed between both hands; then gradually roll these backwards and forwards until they form like a ball; they must be kept united, or they do not uniformly partake of the roll or twist which so prominently distinguishes the *better* teas; although it is difficult at first to keep them united, a little perseverance, with a determination to accomplish the task, will soon enable the tyro to overcome all difficulties. It should however be understood that the *twist* is what is required, the necessary peculiar volution of the hand therefore will be readily understood.

Leaves of sizes should be kept together.

"I would, from experience, here suggest to the planter, that in the periods of gathering, his pickers be divided, according to the number he may have and the size of his plantation. For instance, instead of picking the leaves of all sizes promiscuously and throwing them into one basket, post off your men; if there are fifty engaged for the work, supposing you may desire four sorts of tea, order twelve (marked No. 1,) to bring in Pekoe leaves, twelve more (marked No. 2,) for Souchong, twelve more (marked No. 3,) for Congou, and the remainder (No. 4,) for Bohea, if this latter be wanted, though this class of leaf, by the bye, in Assam is not so easy to manufacture into anything saleable on account of the enormous size of the leaf.

After picking, how to support the plant.

"After a picking, to give vigour to the plant for its next supply of leaves, it becomes necessary to look carefully to its roots. My own practice has been strictly to watch the trees and assist their subsequent produce by not only thorough weeding, but by a gentle hoeing near the roots, and earth thrown up afterwards round the roots to the height of some seven or eight inches. To secure a good crop as well as good produce, I would recommend that the plants (if an artificial plantation) be not sown too near to one another. Where tea is indigenously found, ground is generally, I think, not much in request. One of the Government plantations in Assam, *Chubwa*, is a proof of this assertion; the young suckers and plants not having been removed from around the parent stems, the soil has become exhausted, and but few leaves are obtainable from these. *Pruning* too is absolutely necessary to check the plant, naturally wild, from shooting up beyond picking height, but the most proper time for this I am myself not competent to judge of, although very desirable that it should be ascertained. It is more than probable too that the operation known in horticulture as *stopping*, would be a preferable method of obtaining this object.

Pruning.

Sowing and transplanting.

"In sowing, where you have an abundant supply of seed, I would recommend from two to three to be put three or four inches deep in each hole, at distances of six feet from one another, and at each of these places any particular mark, such as an arrow or piece of stick, should be placed, as in weeding the young plants might stand a chance of being rooted up. This way of planting I have found to be more profitable and to yield ultimate-

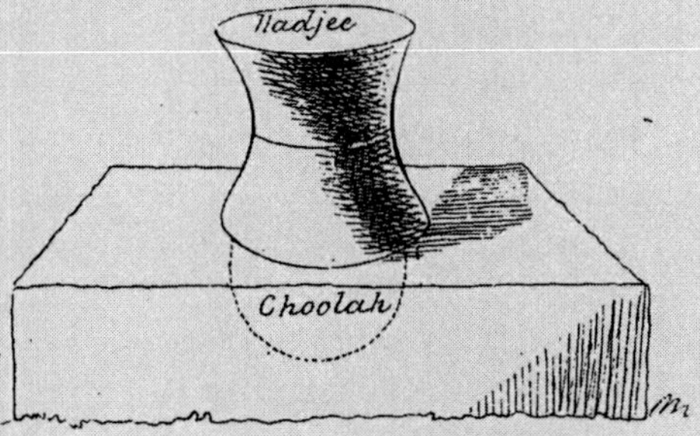

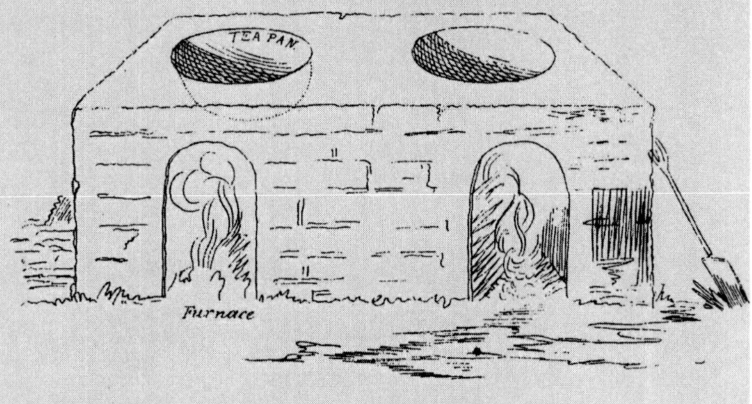

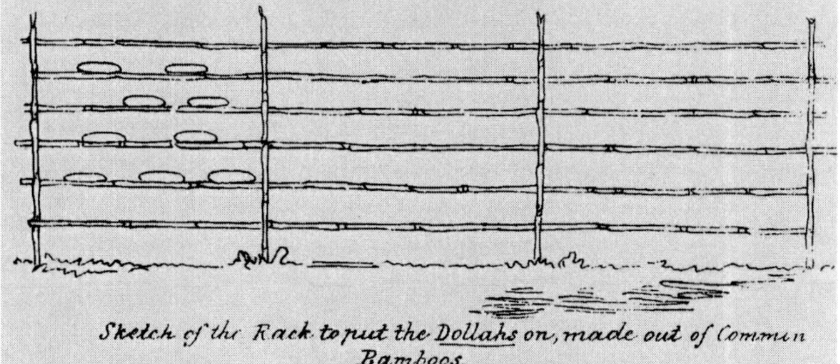

Sketch of the Rack to put the Dollahs on, made out of Common Bamboos.

ly finer trees than those educated in a nursery close together, and afterwards transplanted ; for the spiral root, when taken up even carefully, is slightly damaged, and stunts if not altogether kills the plant.

Miscel-laneous remarks.

" When the shrubs arrive to the height of three feet they should be stopped down to force the stem in throwing out branches laterally and thereby form a bush. Should more than one of the three come up, I would recommend the weaker plants being thrown away. A few days prior to the young leaves appearing on the trees, that is about March, it is advisable to pluck and throw away *all* the old leaves that may be on, taking care that they *are not torn off*, because if this be done the young leaf between the stem and the old leaf may be carried away, and thus harm done by loss of produce. All leaves taken from the plants should be *plucked off* with the thumb and fore finger, leaving the stalk with a small portion of the leaf attached to it.

" After the foregoing data, in which perhaps observations may appear likely to prove of benefit to the planter, I will proceed to notice the different instruments used in the tea house.

Pans.

" *Pans*, (*Koras*,) diameter about two feet, and depth ten inches, with round rims.

Rolling tables.

" *Tables for rolling.*—The best are four feet in breadth, with proportionate length to the size of the plantation, and with reference to height as conveniently for rolling as the size of the people in the province will admit.

Dollahs. " *Dollahs,*—or rounded flat mats for rolling the tea on also, (or those before spoken of) as being three feet in diameter with a two or three inch rim all round.

Challonees. " *Challonees,* for drying the leaves out in the sun. They are of two shapes, one the size of the dollah, the other nearly double. In kind it is more of a sieve than the dollah, which is mat-work, or bamboos laid close together. In the *challonee* each bamboo should be half an inch in breadth, leaving another half inch open (sieve-like) and so on alternately.

Hadjees. " *The hadjee,* also of bamboo *mat*-work, in shape resembling a common *morah,* without a top, and all the inside of it papered. A convenient sized one should be about three and a half feet high, two feet at the extremities, tapering inwards towards the centre, at which place it is about one and a half feet, so as to receive another small sieve.

Small sieve. " *A small sieve,* to fit in the centre of the hadjee, which holds the tea whilst drying over the charcoal fire.

Flue. " *Flue,* a small bamboo one which stands erect in the centre of the *small sieve* in the *hadjee,* a round which the tea is packed.

Sundries. " *Poker, tongs,* and *shovel* for stirring up the fire in the furnaces.

" *Baskets*, of depth, for bringing in the leaves, with a piece of rattan attached for the purpose of slinging it round the neck, that the pickers may command both hands. **Baskets.**

" *Choolas*, or a row of mud recesses for the reception of charcoal, over which the *hadjees* are placed to dry the tea. **Choolas.**

" In picking, the three or four end leaves may be plucked off *with the stalk altogether*, the remaining under ones nipped off at the end *leaving the stalk* on the tree; the former are usually manufactured into Pekoe and Souchong, and the latter into Congou and Bohea. On their being brought in by the pickers to the tea house (if a sunny day) they should be lightly scattered over the *challonees*, and these latter be placed out in the sun on a *machan*, or bamboo framework, which, whether for real use or merely *deknee-ka-wastee*, I do not know, is generally built diagonally. **Manufacture.** **First process.**

" When the stalks of the younger leaves appear faded, perfectly supple, and will bend round, it is time to take them back into the tea house, where they are placed on gratings built on purpose, until they get perfectly cool. They are then brought down, placed on the table and beaten, or rather tossed up between the arms and hands until the serrated *edges* of the leaves have assumed a reddish hue. Put them again in the sun on the *machan* for a short time, and when wearing an increased withered appearance repeat the former operation, that of cooling and beating. Second process. They are now fit for the pan. Prepare your furnaces (*with wood*, not charcoal,) wash your pans well, throw in your leaves, when moderately heated,turning them continually over with your hands or two pieces of wood, taking care to give all as nearly as possible an uniform gradual heat; when no longer bearable to the hand, throw them suddenly out into a *dollah*, which must be ready to receive them, in the hands of one of your artizans, (stationed there for the purpose;) place this on the table, and while hot allow your rollers to take each a handful, and endeavour to give by this operation to the leaf as perceptibly permanent a twist as you possibly can. Ten minutes rolling for young leaves will suffice; the tougher ones proportionately require more. Now scatter as gently as possible, these lumps out on *dollahs*, until the leaves separate without injury to the twist; let them cool, and when perfectly so, introduce them again to the pan to go through a second firing. Roll again on the table, scatter *more* gently out on the *dollahs*, and lay them by on the grating till cool. Then light your *choolahs* with charcoal, taking care that *no* smoke arises from it, and lay thinly on the *small sieves* the leaves which now begin to wear the appearance of tea inside and at the centre of the hadjee; when found to be dry and crisp take them off the fire and lay them by on *dollahs* and on the gratings. This is considered all of the first day's work. In the morning divide your men, half to repeat the foregoing process as directed, and the other half to go on finishing the former day's as I will now direct.

"The fried leaves, it will be recollected, were laid by in *dollahs* on the grating in the tea house. Turn the hands out at daylight, and giving a dollahful to a couple of men, let them pick out and separate all those of corresponding sizes. When this is done light your *choolahs* again, place your *hadjees*, with the *little sieves* over them. Place also the *flue* upright in the centre of the *little sieve*, pack the partially-manufactured leaves of yesterday all round it up to the top of the hadjee, and allow it to remain over the fire (without the instrument receiving even a single shake,) until the leaves gather a sufficient crispness and uniformity of color, by the heat; over slow fires they are sometimes allowed to remain all night, but a practised eye, and attentive watching, can alone determine the precise time of its finish. One circumstance I must not omit, it being one of serious loss if neglected,—the necessity of not even touching the *hadjee* while with tea in it over the fire, lest even one leaf should fall through the sieve and be burned causing smoke, which would of course spoil the whole. When this is cool, pack into your boxes taking care to press the tea down with both feet and hands. Tea in a box when opened ought to be so well packed as to entirely resist the arm when introduced into it.

ZOOLOGY.

Zoology of Assam generally.

But little has hitherto been done towards investigating the Zoology of Assam generally, and none with reference to the hill districts in particular, further than that a few fishes from the mountain streams of the Khassya, Bootan, and Mishmee ranges, are described in McClelland's 'Calcutta Journal of Natural History,' No. 8, page 586 *et seq.* A catalogue of the various specimens procured by the deputation sent by Government to explore the tea districts of Assam, in 1836, is published in the 'Quarterly Journal of the Calcutta Medical and Physical Society' for July 1837 and copied into the 'India Review' for 1838, page 508 *et seq*; but comparing the names of species given in that catalogue, with those of the mammalia and birds collected by Dr. McClelland and his colleagues, as given by Dr. Horsfield in the 'Proceedings of the Zoological Society' for 1839, it would appear that many of those names have been superceded by prior appellations in the latter catalogue, and that, consequently, such species were not regarded as new when examined by scientific naturalists in London. It is to be regretted, however, that Dr. Horsfield's catalogue in the 'Proceedings of the Zoological Society' above refer-

Zoology of Assam generally.

red to, relates only to the class of mammalia, and but to the land or terrene portion of that of birds. The fishes of Assam have been ably and amply treated of by Dr. McClelland, in the second part of the 19th vol. of the 'Asiatic Researches;' and a more complete catalogue of Assamese mammalia has been published by Dr. H. Walker in the 'Calcutta Journal of Natural History,' No. 10, for July 1842. On referring to Mr. Blyth, of the Asiatic Society, for information upon this subject, he obligingly called my attention to the several papers referred to, but especially to the catalogue by Dr. Walker; respecting which he mentioned, however, that he doubted altogether the existence of the European hare (*Lepus timidus*) in the province, conceiving that the animal so termed by Dr. McClelland in the catalogue given by Dr. Horsfield, was no other than the ordinary Bengal hare (*L. ruficaudatus*), which, together with the former, is included by Dr. Walker. He also informed me that I might add the names *Cynopterus marginatus, Meles leucurus, Arctictis binturong*, and *Pteromys magnificus*, to the list, and that *Vulpes bengalensis* is rare and occurs on the plains only.

Respecting the peafowl of Assam, Mr. Blyth also assured me that the bird described in Dr. McClelland's original list is merely the common wild peafowl of Bengal and of India generally, differing in no respect in its colours and markings from an ordinarily coloured tame peafowl in England. But what I have here more properly to treat of, is the Zoology of the Naga ranges of mountains; and I proceed therefore now to offer a few observations of my own on the animal inhabitants of these regions, which have never yet been explored by a scientific Zoologist.

Zoology of the Naga ranges.

Of *Quadrumana*, four species are common.

Hylobates Hoolock. (Hoolock, or black ape.) These animals live in large societies, numbering from about 100 to 150 individuals; and are exceedingly noisy, so much so as to be heard, when in a body, at a distance of some miles. They are easily tamed when taken young, but are difficult to catch, as they usually keep to the tops of the highest Oolung and Mackoi trees, of the fruits of which they are very fond. During the rains, they sip their drink from the leaves of trees, but in the hot season descend frequently to the ravines, dipping their fingers into the water and sipping from them. These animals are not generally supposed to have sufficient courage to attack man, but the following occurrence happened to myself. Upon one occasion, when cutting a road which had been completed from Hookun Joree to a distance of three miles, I was returning the length of this road on foot, when a body of them surrounded me, impelled perhaps as much by curiosity at my European dress and appearance, as by resentment at the intrusion of a stranger upon

Zoology of the Naga ranges.

their domain ; the trees on either side were full of them, menacing with their gestures, and uttering shrill cries ; and as I passed on, several descended from the trees behind, and followed me along the road, and I have no doubt they would have soon attacked me, had not my superior speed on the ground enabled me to escape from them. Having at first to cross a number of felled logs, it was really no easy matter to get away; but the clear and open road once gained, I was not long in distancing my pursuers. It must be remembered, however, that this was a solitary instance, as regards myself, for I have many times come suddenly upon parties of hoolocks, when emerging from a foot-path in the jungle to the open ravines, when the animals were washing and frolicking in the bed of the rapid ; and on such occasions they always made a hasty retreat into the jungle, the moment they caught sight of me. In fact, it is but rarely one can get more than a momentary view of them, except when they are on the tops of the highest trees. Upon my return after the threatened attack of the hoolocks, I sent for my Assamese interpreter, (who thoroughly understood the Naga languages, having been brought up on the hills,) and asked him whether it was usual for these apes to evince so hostile a disposition ; he replied that only a few days before, a party of Nagas were proceeding, necessarily in Indian file (as it is called,) along one of the jungle-paths, when the first of the suite, preceding his companions by some yards, was actually attacked and severely bitten on the shoulder, and would doubtless have been killed by his assailants, had not his followers opportunely come to the rescue, upon the appearance of whom the hoolocks immediately fled. They even seem capable of destroying large snakes; for my attention was once arrested by the noise which a party of hoolocks were making on the tops of some lofty trees overhead, in a plantation which I had the charge of, when, after a while, I was startled by the fall of a Boa snake,* about six or seven feet in length, within a few paces of me. The reptile was nearly dead, or for that matter might have been stunned by the fall, but it was severely bitten and lacerated, no doubt by the hoolocks above, who were unquestionably the cause of its precipitation.

Semnopithecus entellus, (the *Ghora Banor* of the Assamese, or *Hoonuman* monkey of Bengal, with black hands and feet; and which Mr. Blyth has lately shewn to differ from its representative in the peninsula of India;) very common, and found in the same places as the hoolock.

S. pileatus—a monkey, which *I think* I recognize in the species so named by Mr. Blyth, and which that gentleman informs me abounds on the Tipperah hills, retiring far into the interior during the rains, and which therefore

* Termed, *Python tigris* in the Asiatic Society's Museum.

Zoology of the Naga ranges.

may probably extend into the Naga and Abor ranges, is less numerous than either of the foregoing, and is generally observed on or near the ground, especially about the exposed roots of the different species of *Ficus*, upon the fruit of which they subsist in great part. It is considerably smaller than the hoonuman.

Macacus—(?) a small species of this genus of monkeys occurs in great numbers about the beds of the Namsang, Bukloop, and other rapids, where they may often be seen feeding on crabs, and shelled mollusca. They are very sportive in their manners and by no means shy. It appears to be the same species as the Asiatic Society has received from the coast of Arracan, and which is described to have precisely similar habits, keeping to the vicinity of water, and feeding much on shellfish. Two species of this genus are mentioned in Dr. Walker's catalogue of Assamese mammalia, the *M. assamensis*, and *M. rhesus* (or common monkey of the Bengal Soonderbuns.)

Cheiroptera.—Bats would seem to be rare upon these hills; indeed, I do not remember to have noticed any. Even the large flying fox (*Pteropus Edwardsii*), so very numerous in the plains, does not appear to extend to the hill country.

Carnivora.

Canivora.

Felis tigris. (Tiger.)—Not so abundant on the hills as in the plains: although, during the wet season, when the low country is inundated, they make for the nearest hills. The Nagas sometimes convert the skins of these animals into caps.

Leopards are not often seen.

Of the smaller species of *Felis*, I am unable to give any information. A few domestic cats are now and then seen in the Naga villages, but they appear to have been a recent introduction.

Pariah dogs have also found their way to the villages from the plains below: and there is a smaller race on the Abor hills, remarkable for its sagacity, which is employed in hunting as noticed in page 19.

Canis lupus. Wolves abound at the foot of the hills, especially between Tippum and Jaipur, and are very destructive to the cattle of the ryots and residents; but they do not ascend the hill country.

A very few jackals (*Canis aureus*) inhabit some of the ravines: but foxes are altogether wanting, as also hyænas.

Mangusta. Of the mungoose genus, there appear to be two or three species, differing in size, &c. Also different kinds of *Paradoxurus*; and there are otters in the natural reservoirs of water upon the mountains.

Zoology of the Naga ranges.

Bears are wanting : but the Binturong (*Arctictis binturong*) is very abundant.

Of the *Insectivora*, hedgehogs are not uncommon. The Assamese mole I have never remarked.

RODENTIA.

Rodentia.

Squirrels are very numerous, and of many species, differing much in size, and colour. A large kind of rat, probably the bandicoot (*mus giganteus*,) I found very troublesome. On first clearing a piece of ground, and establishing a residence, not any made their appearance for a while, but after a few weeks they began to infest the place in considerable numbers, and were certainly not introduced with any goods, for the simple reason that I had not received any, and I had scarcely anything with me but my guns and my blanket.

Of porcupines, there must be many, and their quills are commonly used for purposes of ornament ; but I never happened to see one. Of hares there do not appear to be any, but these animals require an open country. They abound on the churs of the Bramahpootra, and on the plains of Assam.

EDENTATA.

Edentata.

Manis.—I observed an animal of this genus on the rocky slope of the Namsang rapid, and it is well known to the Nagas, who sometimes spear them for food. From its size, as compared with other species in the Asiatic Society's Museum it is probably the common Indian species, *M. pentadactyla*, which is included in Dr. Walker's catalogue. Zoology of the Naga ranges.

Pachydermata.

Pachydermata.

Elephas indicus.—The hills abound in wild elephants. Habitat—usually near rivers, where a peculiar kind of Terrar grass occurs. They move in large herds, which are decidedly timorous of man. The Nagas eat their flesh, taking the animals by means of pitfalls. Occasionally, too, they are caught both by the stockade method, and by means of trained tame ones; but fifty per cent. of them, die soon after capture. "From seven hundred to a thousand elephants are exported from Assam every year, but the speculation is very precarious. About twice as many as are exported generally die during the process of training, and if to this sum, we add the great number of these animals which are annually killed by the hill tribes for their tusks, we may form some faint idea of the vast multitudes that usually roam in the forests." They are peculiar, however, to the hills, or very nearly so. The young, from two to two and a half feet high have often been brought to me, but I was never able to keep them alive more than five or six days.

The rhinoceros does not inhabit the hills, the natives procuring parts of the skin of this animal, which is held in high estimation for

Zoology of the Naga ranges. breastplates, by barter with the people of the plains.

Pachydermata. Wild hogs are exceedingly abundant, and their traces are to be met with everywhere. Tame pigs are also bred, in great numbers in the Naga village, passing the night under the *machans* (or raised houses,) and finding their own subsistence in the jungle. Both wild and tame occasion much inconvenience where there is any cultivation. Notwithstanding that the mode of life of the tame race so nearly resembles that of the wild, it is curious that the former are very degenerated, being much smaller, and they also vary in colour as usual among domesticated animals, being either black, white, or pied. They are never emasculated. The Naga mode of killing these animals is worthy of remark: the pig is held fast, and a pointed piece of wood is driven into the spiral chord immediately behind the skull.

Ruminantia.

Ruminantia. *Cervidæ* or Deer. The *Saumer*, or *Elk* of Europeans *Cervus hippelaphus*,—or perhaps, from the magnitude of its horns, it may be the Himalayan *Jerów* (*C. Aristotelis*),—occurs in large herds, more particularly about the vicinity of the brine-springs. Neither the spotted nor the hog deer (*C. axis* and *C. porcinus*) appear to inhabit the hills. The Muntjac, or barking deer, is very numerous; but no species of

Chevrotain, or mouse deer, occurs to my knowledge. Zoology of the Naga ranges.

Rumi-nantia.

Capridæ. A domestic breed of goats, with long hair in the males, much shorter in the females, is reared in great numbers both by the Nagas and the Abors, who occasionally kill them for food, but never milk them, these tribes having a prejudice against the milk of any animal, which they regard as an excrement. The horns, when polished, are converted into ear-ornaments; and the hair of the males, which is from four to five inches long, is used to decorate their caps, spears, and battle-axes. The males are much esteemed by the people of the plains to cross with the common domestic goats of the low country. Sheep they have none, nor are there any in Assam, besides the few that have been carried up by Europeans. Of wild species, there is a small black animal, nearly allied to the *Goral* of the Himalaya, and which is perhaps the *Antelope goral* of Dr. Walker's list, (possibly thus identified from the horns only), which is confined to bold rocky situations, and is extremely difficult of access, or even to get a sight of, keeping as it does to places which, for the most part, are inaccessible to man. It is a most agile creature, which I have only seen on two or three occasions at a distance, and could never get a shot at: but I have had both the heads and skins brought to me, which latter were covered with short soft hair, of a deep glossy black colour; this at once distinguishing it from the Himalayan Goral, while the character of the hair is very different from that of the shaggy *Næmorhædus* group, exemplified by the Himalayan *Surów*.

Bovidæ. The humped cattle of India, and also the buffalo, have but recently been introduced upon these hills, where a few of the latter are now bred by the Nagas. It is remarkable that these are already much finer than the buffaloes of the plains, which I attribute to the circumstance of the Nagas not milking their cattle, from the notion already stated, but allowing the calves to derive their full amount of nutriment from the mother; and if this be the true reason, it will also explain why the tame buffaloes of India, generally, are so much smaller, upon the average, than the wild ones, although they resort to the same localities, and would appear to lead as nearly the same life as possible. The indigenous domestic cattle of these hills is the *Mit'hun*, or *Gayal* (*Bos frontalis*), which is now becoming scarce, probably from their having been killed and eaten faster than the breed could be kept up, now that there is a facility of obtaining buffaloes from the plains to supply their place. They are extremely gentle, and, though docile, slow in their movements; and their colour is often pied. They do not now occur wild upon these hills, nor could I hear of any other species of wild cattle; though I perceive that the head of a female *Gaour* (*Bos gaurus*, erroneously termed *Bison* by Indian sportsmen), and which is also a hill species, has been recently forwarded by Major Jenkins to the Asiatic Society's Museum. Zoology of the Naga ranges.

BIRDS.

Birds.

In this class, I will not venture to specify in detail, as I have with the mammalia: nor would it be easy to procure a large proportion of the birds of these hills, as the canopy of foliage over-head is so loftily raised, that the species which inhabit it can scarcely be even seen, and are generally beyond the reach of shot. One of the most conspicuous birds of these vast forests, from the noise which it makes at certain seasons, is the great *Buceros cavatus*, or *Homrai* of Mr. Hodgson, the voice of which conveys the idea of the felling of timber, and has more than once led me to suppose that a party of Nagas were at work. Woodpeckers are very numerous, and of many species: and of those birds which frequent the ground and its vicinity, the most abundant appears to be identical with the common *Saatbhye* or *chatarrhœa* of Bengal (*Malacocercus terricolo*), so well known from its familiarity and harsh chattering cries. The Hill Mynah (*Gracula religiosa*) is also of frequent occurrence, more particularly among the Abors.

Of the *Gallinaceæ*, the wild Peafowl (*Pavo cristatus*, not *P. muticus*,) abounds chiefly in

Zoology of the Naga ranges.

Birds.

the vicinity of rice cultivation, being never molested by the natives, who regard it with a certain veneration. Jungle-fowls (*Gallus bankivus*) are also very numerous, especially near water; and the *Deo-derrick*, or purple pheasant of the hill districts of Assam (*Eupvocomus Cuvieri*), is likewise common, being seldom seen to fly, but upon alarm running away fast among the underwood. I know of no other species of this tribe. Domestic fowls have been lately introduced from the plains; and as the Nagas eat only of the flesh of the male (as already mentioned), it is probable that they will soon become abundant. The flesh of ducks they reject altogether, and often expressed their wonder at my raising a few for my own table.

Reptiles.

Reptiles.

A species of *Varanus* is common, and I am not aware that it ever enters the water, but it often ascends trees; it attains to about three feet in length; and the skin only, after being first dried in the sun, and then crisped over a fire, is commonly eaten by the Nagas. Snakes are abundant, and of very many species, from the large *Phython tygris*, which I have seen fully thirty feet in length, to the small worm-like *Typhlops;* but as accidents seldom happen from them, I infer that but a small proportion of them are venomous. The *Cobra* I never observed. The Nagas eat indiscriminately of all, cooking them as already stated.

Zoology of the Naga ranges.

Fishes, &c.

Fishes.

There are several good edible fishes in the Naga streams, but I do not feel myself competent to speak of them: and the same remark will apply to the non-vertebrated animals generally. To the entomologist, in particular, these regions offer a most ample and inviting field for research, as nothing can exceed the variety and beauty of the insect tribes which swarm in every district and kind of locality. The extraordinary leaf-insect (*Phyllium siccifolium,*) as it is badly called, for the appearance of the living insect is that of a green and healthy leaf), is far from being rare; and brilliant glow-worms and fire-flies of different species embellish both the ground and foliage when the diurnal tribes have gone to their repose. In short, to the naturalist, the hill regions of Assam constitute a region of the highest promise, which it is much to be wished that some competent observer might have the opportunity of turning to due account. Mr. Hodgson has done much towards the investigation of the Zoology of Nepal, and Captain Phayre is now exerting himself, with considerable success, in the elucidation of the fauna of Arracan. Messrs. Blyth and McClelland have likewise made great progress in determining the animals of Lower Bengal: and there are other equally successful students of Zoology in Southern India: but

Zoology of the Naga ranges.

Fishes.

Assam has yet to look forward to the time when a resident naturalist shall labour to make known its rich stores, abundant as they are in all that can interest the lover of natural history, and almost unexplored as these stores have hitherto been.

MISCELLANEOUS.

It has been before noticed, in page 11, that the unmarried men are not allowed to sleep under the parental roof, if female relations dwell in the same abode: but in every village there is a *Morang*, or large house, with high gable ends and eaves reaching down to the ground; and inside this building are a series of bamboo bed-places covered with coarse mats elevated two or three feet from the ground, and upon which the young men repose. They rise early and usually retire from eight to nine o'clock in the evening. In one of these *Morangs*, the writer of this has slept. **Miscellaneous.**

With the exception of one or two individuals, who remain on guard all night, and make a little noise, the place was very quiet until sunrise, when we were awakened by a shrill scream from the party on guard, in which all soon joined. It may be imagined that I was a little startled, and my first impulse was to look for my gun. It appeared, however, upon enquiry, that it was merely the customary morning call, for each to pursue his respective occupation. A descent to the rapid below immediately followed this call, and in less than five minutes not a single person was to be seen. The guard is *always* stationed during the night on a high perch, overtopping

Miscellaneous. all the houses ; and the punishment is very severe when any remissness of duty is detected. In case of fire in a neighbouring village, or signs of an attack in any shape, a pass-word is given, and every man is instantly on his legs, carrying his battle-axe and spear ; and a large hollow tree, which is invariably kept in the *Morang*, is struck by large pieces of wood, which noise, in the dead of night, may well be imagined to rouse up the whole village. The brief period of time in which they all muster is incredible. The kind of tree referred to is, of itself, when scooped out, capable of producing a tremendous noise, and is on certain occasions used as a musical instrument. On the young men attaining the age of manhood, or when about twenty years of age, they are tatooed, declared servants of the chief, also eligible for marriage, and are compelled to wrestle with, and often to fight with weapons, a corresponding sized villager. About noon, they usually all returned to the village, bringing in burdens of salt, wood, vegetables, grain, &c.

In former times, the brutal attacks of these people on one another were savage in the extreme. Mr. Robinson gives an account of such mode of warfare. Even in their hottest and most active wars, they proceed wholly by stratagem, and ambuscade. They see no merit in attacking their enemies with open force. To surprise and destroy is the greatest glory of a commander and the highest pride of his followers. If no straggling parties can be intercepted, they advance towards the villages, and if so fortunate as to remain unobserved, they fire the enemy's huts in the dead of night, and massacre the inhabitants as they fly defenceless from the plains. When the enemy is caught unprepared, they rush upon them with the utmost ferocity, and tear off the scalps of as many as fall victims to their rage. These strange trophies of their triumph they carry home, and preserve as monuments not only of their prowess, but of the vengeance which they have inflicted upon the people who were objects of public resentment. On the death of a warrior, all the scalps taken by him during his lifetime are burnt with his remains. Miscellaneous.

Such a mode of warfare may be attributed to a feeble and dastardly spirit, incapable of generous or manly exertion; but when it is considered that many of these tribes, upon occasions which call for extraordinary efforts, not only defend themselves with obstinate resolution, but attack their enemies with the most daring courage, and that they possess fortitude of mind superior to the sense of danger, or the fear of death, we must ascribe this habitual caution to some other cause than constitutional timidity. The number of men in each tribe is so small and the difficulty of rearing new members amidst the hardships and dangers of savage life is so Mode of warfare.

Miscellaneous. great, that the life of a citizen is extremely precious, and the preservation of it becomes a main object in their policy. Had the point of honor been the same amongst the feeble Naga tribes as among the powerful nations of Europe; had they been taught to court fame and victory, in contempt of danger and death, they must have been ruined by motives so ill adapted to their condition. But wherever their communities are more populous, so that they can act with considerable force, and can sustain the loss of several of their number without being sensibly weakened, the military operations of the Nagas more resemble those of other nations. They openly defy their enemies to the combat, engage in regular battles, and maintain the conflict with that desperate ferocity which is natural to men who, having no idea of war but that of extermination, never give, or take quarter.

Absence of temples, priests, &c. "Idols, temples, priests and mythological writings, which in the eyes of an unenlightened people make error venerable and aid to perpetuate superstition through successive ages, do not exist among the Nagas."

Dancing. "Among rude tribes in every part of the globe, the love of dancing is a favorite passion, and we find it to be the same case with the Nagas. As during a great part of their time, they languish in a state of inactivity and indolence without any occupation to rouse or interest them, they delight universally in a pastime which calls forth the active powers of their nature into exercise. All the Naga dances are imitations of some action, and though the music by which they are regulated is extremely simple and tiresome to the ear by its dull monotony, some of their dances appear wonderfully expressive and animated. Their war-dance is perhaps the most striking. In this, the women dance in an inner circle, whilst the men holding up their weapons in their hands dance round them, beating time, and singing in strains of wild and plaintive melody. They move in slow and decent movements, but the men, arrayed in their full war dress, enter with enthusiastic ardour into their several parts; they exhaust themselves by perpendicular jumps and side leaps, in which they exhibit considerable agility. On the whole their gestures, their countenances, and their voices are exceedingly wild, and well adapted to their various situations." Miscellaneous.

Many attempts have been, and are now being made to trace Buddhism from Bengal into China through the Eastern districts. That it was not through the Naga states is evident, for they have neither written character, priests nor temples. It was no doubt through Bootan and Llassa, as it is to this day, and that Buddhism prevailed in Assam, there can be no reasonable doubt. The Thibetians have a record as mentioned by M. Csomo de Koros that their last Buddh studied or meditated at Hajoo, and it Attempts to trace Buddhism from Bengal into China thro these regions.

Miscellaneous. is in connection with this tradition no doubt that Hajoo is even still a place of pilgrimage to the *Booteahs* and *Tibetians*, from every part of Tibet and Tartary, and perhaps to *Chinese*, for many of the pilgrims are Chinese in dress, and besides, there is no old temple in Assam that is not standing on, or built with the remnants, and materials of older temples, which must have been Buddh temples, destroyed when Brahminism became rampant. That Brahminism is of young date in Assam we may be certain from all the Brahmin families tracing their descent from Brahmins invited in by the Rajahs from *Kanour* and *Nuddeah*, and that only a few generations ago with the most ancient families: add to this that all the oldest temples now existing are held by *Soodurs*, and, not by *Brahmins*.

Political relations, &c. It would be tedious to enter into all our negociations with the Nagas *generally*, but the causes for, and the results of the different deputations towards interference may be briefly stated.

The first expedition made was that of Mr. Grange in 1839 to the Angami Nagas, of which an account has been published in the Journal of the Asiatic Society.

These Nagas, a very powerful tribe, who opposed Colonel Pemberton and Major Jenkins in their march through their country in 1831-32, and long been very troublesome to the villagers in the northern hills of Cachar. Capt. Burns, the superintendent, having been unable to restrain them and their murderous attacks, threatening to depopulate the whole of the Cachar hills, the British Government was called upon to punish them, supposing them under its control: but as they were not in any way connected with Assam then, Major Jenkins proposed that Northern Cachar should be transferred to us, when it was hoped these savages might be brought to their senses. The hills were transferred, and after successive deputations of Capt. Bigge and Mr. Grange in 1839-40, 40-41, 41-42 and 42-43 (in the cold seasons,) the chiefs after some small punishment, conciliation, and management were at last prevailed on to attend at Nowgong in 1843, and then entered into engagements of allegiance and promises to abstain from any attacks on British subjects, or on Naga tribes connected with us. From the return of their villages, and houses, a census was computed as regards population of full 60,000 persons. They have not exactly remembered all their engagements, but since Mr. Grange's first deputation they have not molested any of our villages, and no atrocity has been traced to them.

Miscellaneous.

Political relations.

The Cachar tribes, which were in a bad state, are now fast recovering, and from a nominal revenue of 900 rupees have increased to a net revenue of 1900 rupees and are likely quickly to

Miscellaneous. improve from numbers of *Kukis* coming across from the Tipperah hills and settling in Northern

Political relations. Cachar.

The Angami Nagas will themselves prove good and useful allies by and bye, commercially and otherwise, but our trade is as yet small, and indeed confined to twelve maunds of tea seeds which Messrs. Wood and Herring got from them for salt and beads last season. This tribe had for ages carried on a trade with the Bengallees of Sylhet in slaves, and all their depredations had the carrying off of slaves in view, which is entirely put a stop to.

Our first acquaintance with the Eastern Nagas arose out of our rights in the salt wells. When the British Government received the province from Poorundur-duter, all the hauts were levied in a very oppressive way. One-seventh of all the goods brought for the purchase of salt was received by the Government, and one-fourth of all brought down was also taken. There was besides a large establishment who plundered all the trades on their own account. It immediately confined its demands to twenty per cent. of the salt brought down, which gave it a clear revenue of 1600 rupees and upwards.

Mr. Strong, in the cold season of 1839-40, was sent up to make a report on all the wells, and to suggest any alteration in the duties which might appear necessary. This gentleman reported eighty-five salt wells belonging to the

Nam Sangeeas, Panneedwar, and Bardwar Nagas, in all which, with one or two exceptions, Government had an equal share. The result of Mr. Strong's tour was the abolition of all duties, similar ones having before been abolished throughout Assam.

Miscellaneous.

Political relations.

In 1841-42 Captain Brodie was deputed to visit all the Eastern Nagas from the *Dekho* to the *Boree Deehing* rivers, and to bring them to terms. This arose out of murders in the dwars of our subjects, for which we could get no satisfaction. Captain Brodie's expedition was very successful; he traversed all the hills of the Boree Nagas, received their submission and engagements not to attack our people, and to refer to our Government all disputes between themselves and with the Abor Nagas and the result has been very satisfactory. They have in general abstained from all offences towards us, and those continual exterminating wars between themselves have almost entirely ceased.

During the same season Captains Vetch and Lloyd visited the Naga tribes, east of the Boree Deehing for the purpose of relieving them from the thraldom of the Singphoes, and these gentlemen had interviews with all the Naga chiefs in that direction.

This last season Captain Brodie explored the country of the Nagas from the *Dekho*, to the *Dhunsiri*, and entered into engagements with all the chiefs in connexion with Assam, to the same

Miscellaneous.

Political relations.

effect as with the Eastern Nagas, but it is feared these tribes are likely to turn out a more intractable race than those more eastward. Their habits are less industrious; they are more given to drunkenness, and the power of the chiefs appears to be very limited indeed. These tribes are very numerous and some of their villages very large. Captain Brodie's report has recently been received by Mr. Secretary Currie, with a map by Mr. Bedford.

It is possible that a deputation will again visit these hills during the approaching cold season, Captain Brodie's last visit having been hurried from the lateness of the season, and badness of the weather, and in consequence left much undone: we have besides a demand to make on them, a party of Nagas having lately attacked and plundered a party of Assamese elephant-hunters killing two of the party, and another gang from the same direction have sacked a Naga village on our immediate frontier. This renders another visit necessary. But ultimately with a little exertion, and a little coaxing the authorities will no doubt reduce them to good order, and this effected, all the Naga tribes on our frontier will have been reduced to submission from Cachar to the Singphoes hills.

The tribes immediately connected with us amount to probably 200,000 people, and as the country behind them of the Abor Nagas is apparently still more thickly peopled, we shall

have no small object if we succeed in effectually preserving tranquillity throughout this fine mountain range. The population has hitherto been greatly kept down by their perpetual wars with each other, and it will no doubt greatly increase if we are able to preserve the peace, and, what must follow, compel the Nagas to become an agricultural and trading race.

Miscellaneous.

Political relations.

The barter carried on now is not altogether trifling, the Eastern Nagas bringing down salt; the Western cotton in large quantities, and all carrying on no small traffic in chillies, cuchoos, &c. &c. for rice, salt and other products. The object of compelling them to acknowledge our supremacy is solely to save our own subjects from aggression, and to put an end to their exterminating attacks on each other, arising out of feuds of blood; these can only be stopped by the interposition of a power superior to their own. Government do not seek to interfere with their external governments, nor have they any idea of imposing any assessments on them. The end will no doubt be a large trade for the valley, and the hills have products mutually necessary to the inhabitants of each.

Supposed junction of the Irrawaddee & T'Sanpo near these hill tribes.

As every cold weather we progress further amongst the hill tribes eastward, we may look forward to more news concerning the long undecided question of the junction between the Irrawaddee and T'Sanpo.

The subject of any connection existing be-

Miscellaneous.

Junction of the Irrawaddee & T'Sanpo near these hill tribes.

tween the T'Sanpo, or Yarou-dzanbotchou of Thibet, the Irrawaddee or Pin-langkiang of Burmah, and the Bramahpootra, or Bor-Lohit of Assam, has for many years afforded matter for Asiatic geographical discussion; and although from nearly every traversable quarter proximate to the country of supposed junction, we are assured that the two former are one and the same river, the statement appears so doubtful, that it merits further enquiry.

Not excepting Klaproth, the well known Thibetian traveller, no mention has ever been made or description offered of the country lying between the parallels of 95° and 96° East longitude, and 25° to 29° North latitude, which is the supposed north and south line where the union forms; but to the north-eastward of this unknown region the country is partially explored; to the westward we find the travels of Wilcox, Pemberton, and others; and to the southward, Captain Hannay's route on the eastern frontier. We may therefore assume that the principal communications on the subject have emanated either from our Politicals on the North Eastern Frontier, who have gathered rude information from Singphoe and Kampti Chiefs, or from Chinese and Tartar surveys.

Contiguous in every quarter to this unexplored country are mountains of considerable height, running in easterly and westerly directions; and inferring from this fact that the *line*

of these formations is not disturbed between the unknown parallels, we may safely arrive at the conclusion that the T'Sanpo and the Irrawaddee are two distinct and separate rivers; the direction wanted to unite them being a north and south one, and the mountainous line preventing it, being an east and west one. Even Chinese curiosity has not as yet explored this country, and no information whatever is to be found from their records as to whether it is inhabited or not. Supposing that a junction existed, the tremendous discharge of waters, tumbling from the ravines, waterfalls and reservoirs on the tops of adjacent mountains, and forming tributaries to the main stream would, when meeting the Irrawaddee, so swell that at present nearly languid current, as to cause a perpetual inundation, and instead of cultivated fields and villages in the neighbourhood of *Bammo*, we should find a labyrinth of rivers, perhaps interposed with large lakes.

Miscellaneous.

Junction of the Irrawaddee & T'Sanpo near these hill tribes.

The direction it pursues will not be an easy matter to ascertain for some time to come; in a country so mountainous and interspersed with rivers, it may likely enough take a course into Tartary; but there is not the slightest reason to doubt that many of the tributary hill streams of the Bramahpootra are fed by tributaries again of the T'Sanpo—for amongst the Mishmee and Singphoe hills eastward, the streams are innumerable, and close to the *Djamga* temple, which is nearly on the banks of that large river. As-

Miscellaneous. samese tradition recognizes the waters of the Bramahpootra flowing from some larger one out of their territory, and supported by information to the same effect from the *Beesa Gaum*, a most powerful, and daring Singphoe chief, all doubts on both subjects may perhaps be considered removed ;- that the T'Sanpo and the Irrawaddee are *not* one and the same river, but that the Bramahpootra is partly fed by waters from the T'Sanpo.

Junction of the Irrawaddee & T'Sanpo near these hill tribes.

Opium. The subject of opium has of late years attracted much attention amongst the moralists and commercial classes in Great Britain; much has been said of the immorality of its use, its destructive effects on the people using it, and the necessity of a Christian Government interfering to prevent its extension, and to discourage such a cultivation. I am not going to enter upon a discussion of these points of the question, nor to argue the propriety or otherwise of prohibiting its production; or of opposing its use; whilst that of malt, and other articles, the pabula of distilled and intoxicating liquors, are encouraged; but it may not be uninteresting to refer to the mode of collecting the juice of the opium plant in *the Naga hills*.

I have no data on which to ground any statistical remarks as to the extent of culture existing on them. Its growth is necessarily limited, on account of its late introduction amongst them by the Assamees.

The course of cultivation of the plant differs little from that pursued in the plains, and when the capsule of the poppy approaches maturity, irregular incisions are made on them with their daw, the exuded matter being collected on strips of cloth, which when perfectly saturated, are rolled into balls, and thus made use of.

Miscellaneous.

Opium.

I am not aware whether the opium so collected has ever been submitted to a chemical test, so as to fix in any manner the difference of value between this and the Government opium. In the form I have described, it is called by the Assamese and Nagas *kani;* with the former it is considered that a piece of the cloth from five to six inches square, infused in water, is one dose, of which from five to six doses are daily taken by those who indulge in it, the cloth being afterwards used in chewing or introduction by the nostrils, and not unusually in their infatuation for the drug, placing it in the orifices of the lobes of their ears. In preparing it for inhalation, some *támul pát* or betel leaves are boiled, dried, and mixed with the opium, the composition being afterwards made into small balls and placed in the *chillum*, a few whiffs of which throw the inhaler in a short time into a state of delightful insensibility, of the pleasure whereof every Assamese opium smoker speaks with the highest gratification—but the Naga used it very cautiously.

Taken to excess, this drug is no doubt debilitating, and injurious to a degree, whilst its mo-

Miscellaneous. Opium. derate use can have little effect on the system, compared with any immoderate indulgence of spirituous liquors; but this is for moralists, not for travellers to speculate on, whilst the duty on consumption usually levied on it in Assam, in common with other articles of production, is of some value to the Government; legitimate, as affecting an object of luxury and indulgence, in common with all excise imposts.

Gold-washing. The following is the Native account of washing for gold in Assam, drawn up by Moneeram, Revenue Sheristadar, Bur Bundaree, and communicated by Capt. F. Jenkins to the Coal and Mineral Committee of the Asiatic Society.

"There are no old papers of the *Assam* time relative to the above subject, but the following is compiled from the statements of respectable people, and shews the present method of gold-washing in this country.

"Before the British took possession of this country, the *Assam* rajas took from the sonwals of *Upper Assam* a yearly tribute of 4000 tolahs of gold, and in the time of the Boora Gohynes 2000 tolahs were taken: when the Government had possession of *Upper Assam*, a tax was levied on the north bank of the river from 400 sonwal pykes, and at present there are about 150 or 160 gotes of pykes in all *Upper Assam*, from whom the raja collects a tax. Besides these there are about 250 or 300 of these pykes (old and new) in the *Bur Senaputtee's* country.

There are also about 10 or 15 gotes* of these sonwals in *Bishnath*, and *Sonaree Chopree*; and some in *Lithure*, *Gorokhia*, *Kalaneecholee*, and *Morung*, and there are 50 or 60 houses of them in *Sadiya* and *Soeekhown*. In the raja's country the greatest number of his sonwal pykes reside on the north bank of the *Bramahpootra*: there are only about 26 houses of them on the south bank. **Miscellaneous.** **Gold-washing.**

Assamese sonwal pykes during the time of Government.	Gotes.	During the present raja's time.	Living now and on which bank of river.	Runaway sonwal pykes where living.
Bur Burooah's Bhag,...	1	,,	,,	Muttuck.
Seering Phookun's Bhag,	29	16½	South bank	,,
Tupomeea Phokun's Bhag,	6½	,,	,,	Muttuck
In Seesee Tangonee, ...	26	,,	,,	Ditto
In Lokimpoor, Soalpanee, Nomel and Charengee Burooah's Bhag,..................	69	44	North bank	,,
In Bunscotta, ...	12½	7	Ditto	,,
In Narainpoor, ...	8	3	Ditto	
Cackaree sonwals, in Seesee, Lokimpoor and Majalee,	250	90	Ditto	Muttuck, &c.
Cackaree sonwals on the south bank, ...	11	4	South bank	,, ,,
Near the Dehing river,..	,,	15	Ditto	,,
Beheea sonwals, ...	44	5	North bank	Muttuck.
	457¼	184½		

"The kheldars object to the 104½ gotes of pykes at present put down by the raja, but admitting all their objections, there are not less than 150 gotes of these sonwal pykes in the raja's country.

"Gold-washing is the occupation of the sonwal pykes, but other pykes sometimes join with them and receive their share. The tax is levied on the

* A gote of sonwals consists of four pykes or individuals.

Miscellaneous. Gold-washing.

sonwals only at the following rates. At the time of the washing, the Burahs, and Sykeas with their sonwal pykes go in a body to the place selected by them, and at the close of the year each pyke gives half a tolah of gold for his share of tax; but there is an extra tax levied for melting, &c. according to the quality of the gold; *for the best kind* (*or votom*) they give three rattees more than the half tolah, for second best (*or modom*) four rattees, for third sort (*or norrem,*) six rattees or one anna; besides this there is a commission of one rupee's weight in every twenty taken by the Phookuns and Burrooahs, half a tolah in twenty by the Teklahs and Burahs, a quarter tolah by the Bhundar Kagotee, and when the tax in gold is presented to the raja, the Chung Kagotee, the Bhundaree Leekeerah, the Pachonee, and the Kookoorah chowah Burah, take altogether one and a quarter tolahs of silver for each tolah of gold.

" In the time of raja Rajeswur Sing, the sonwals of *Upper Assam alone* used to give 6 or 7000 tolahs of gold in addition to the moheea or tax that was levied on them, and in raja Goureenath Sing's time the sonwals of *Upper Assam* used to give 4000 tolahs of gold every year; besides this there was gold received from the following places of *Lower Assam*, *Chingah*, *Sondhonee*, *Chooteea*, and *Chatgarree*, and it was also brought from the Bhooteahs by a *sunzattee*, sent by the raja. The best kind of gold is that found by the jungle sonwals, and the Kacharee sonwals' gold is the worst. Miscellaneous.

"The hill streams produce the best gold, and the stronger the current of the stream the better the gold; very slow running streams do not produce good gold. The gold found in the *Bramahpootra* is not good, it is washed by the Kacharee sonwals, and this is the reason why the Kacharee sonwals have no good gold. Gold-washing.

List of rivers in Assam which produce gold.

1 Lohit	*1 Kakoee	1 Sonsiri	1 *Doka Jooree*
1 Dihing	*1 Kuddum	*1 Jongloong	In the east 2 Jooree, if the gold is washed with consent of the Dufla, each party can collect ¼ tolah daily.
1 Tengapanee	*1 Somdiri	*1 Jajee	
1 Paroorah	*1 Doosra Deejoo	*1 *Desoee*	
1 Dehong and Dibong	1 Dikrung	Under the Dufla hills in Chardoar.	
1 Deegaree	1 Kharaee		
1 Dhol	1 Boorooee	1 Doobeea	1 Pomahs
*1 Seedang	1 Bor Gang	1 Pormaee	1 Garroah
1 Dibooroo	1 Bor Deekoree	1 Roydeng	Besides the above there are several other small streams.
1 Soobun siri	*1 Bhoirobbee	1 Bechumae	
1 Deejoo	1 Mansiri	1 Kallee Jooree	

☞ The names of rivers marked thus* produce the best gold.

"There are other rivers falling into these which produce gold, but the best gold is found in the most winding streams with the strongest currents.

"Not having any old papers on this subject there may be some trifling errors in the above estimates, but it is a positive fact that 4000 tolahs of gold at the very least were received annually by the *Assam* raja.

"There are four methods of collecting gold as follows:—

"1. The Kacharees wait until the river rises, and when it falls again suddenly they scrape up the sand and wash for gold.

"2. All other sonwals collect and wash for gold during the dry season.

Miscellaneous.

Gold-washing.

"3. The sonwal of the Rydegeea Phookun's Bhag go up into the hills and collect the copat, which they burn to produce gold.

"4. The gold-washers in the *Seedang* river get the gold by washing the moss and slime which they scrape off the *rocks* in the bed of the river.

"These are the four methods by which gold is collected, but the gold-washers generally collect the gold during the dry season.

Method of washing and collecting gold from sand.

"Wherever the current is strong with a falling bank above it ending in a sharp turn of the river, the sonwals examine the opposite shore where the sand from the falling bank is thrown, and if this should contain gravel mixed with the sand it is accounted a good place to find gold in.

"Each party consists of a patoee and four pallees, who wash in one trough (or dorongee No. 5); when they find a proper place to commence operations they begin by working about in the sand with a sharp pointed bamboo (No. 1, or sokalee) to find the depth at which the gravelly sand is, they then take it up in a piece of split bamboo, (No. 2, bans chola) and examine whether there is any gold dust in it; if they see twelve or fourteen bits they immediately build their houses and commence operations. They first bund up the deep part of the stream, if it be a small one with sand, and if large with stakes and grass:

the stream then takes a different direction over the sand; they allow it to wash away the upper surface of sand so as to expose the gold sand, when the bund is re-opened and the stream returns to its original bed. The upper sand is then scraped off and the good sand collected with a kind of wooden spade (No. 3, kater dohtal); this shovel is one and a half cubits long by one cubit in breadth, with a handle four cubits long; the blade is of the form of a crescent with holes at each corner through which a string is passed and two men lay hold of and pull this string, while a third person keeps pressing the spade down in a perpendicular position; the sand is then taken up in small baskets with handles (No. 4 called cookees) and thrown on a bamboo lattice work or strainer (No. 6 ban), which is laid over the trough by a dorongee (No. 5.) This trough is made of wood and three cubits long, one cubit broad and one span high all round, with a slit three fingers wide at one end. Water is now thrown over the sand with a calabash having a large piece scooped out at the bottom, beside a very small hole on one side (No. 7, lao;) the water is thrown on with one hand while the other hand is employed in moving the sand about and sweeping off the larger particles of gravel from the surface of the strainer; in this way the sand is spread on and water poured over it; and as the trough fills the water and dirty sand run off through the slit in it, while the clean sand and gold remain at the bottom of the

Miscellaneous.

Gold-washing.

Miscellaneous.

Gold-washing.

trough. I forgot to say that the trough is placed at a small angle to assist the water and dirt to run off quickly. When forty or fifty baskets of sand have been thus washed into the trough the sonwals call it a sheea, and if a ruttee of gold is produced from one sheea they think themselves very fortunate indeed, for during the long days they get above thirty sheeas or washings, producing one ruttee each, and during the short days about twenty-five sheeas, each party thus making on an average about quarter of a tolah of gold daily. When they happen to fall on a good old stream that has not been disturbed for five or six years they get two ruttees of gold from every sheea or washing, and then each party makes about half a tolah daily.

The gold and sand of the last washing is collected into pottles (or chongas) by spreading a leaf of copat or some other plant at the end of the trough, and dropping water very gently on the sand through the small hole in the calabash, which causes a parting of sands and gold to be thrown on the leaf; when the whole is collected in this way it is put into the pottle and tied up and the next washing is commenced on. As soon as they have collected enough in the pottles they give up washing the common sand, but pour out the gold and sand from pottles into the trough again, and putting in about an anna's weight of quicksilver for each tolah of gold dust, they pour water over the sand to keep it in motion, while the quicksilver remains below with the gold dust, and forms it into a lump; this lump is then put into a shell and on a fire of nahor wood charcoal; when the quicksilver evaporates, and the shell becomes lime, it is then carefully taken up in a spoon and thrown into water, when the gold falls to the bottom; if it be of a brass colour, it is wrapped in a paste made of clay from the cooking choolas, mixed with a little salt, and burnt in a fire, which gives it a proper colour.* Miscellaneous. Gold-washing.

"The gold is washed for in all streams during the months of Maug, Falgoon, and Choit, and also in a few streams in the month of Assin and Cartick; but during four days in each, the sonwals do no work, viz. at the new and full of the moon: on the first of the month, and on a general holiday, all natives have *once*, a month called *ekadosee* (the 11th.)

"The Kacharee sonwals use the same instruments as above.

"The Rydengeea Phookun's sonwals burn the copot leaf, and thus produce gold from the ashes as above remarked.

"The gold-washers in the *Seedang* dry the moss and slime, and then wash it in the usual manner.

* This process causes an absolute refinement of the surface of the gold:— it is the same used in gold refining by the natives, but in the latter case the metal has to be reduced in the first instance to very thin leaves to allow the muriatic acid fumes to penetrate and unite with the alloy.

Miscellaneous.

Gold-washing.

This is the way in which gold is washed, which is so uncertain, that an unfortunate set of men sometimes get only about a tolah after a whole month's labor."

I have met with some further information on the gold-washings of Assam, in Capt. Hannay's communications to Capt. Jenkins, Agent to the Governor-General in Assam:

"It is the general belief of the inhabitants of the surrounding countries, that the rivers of the valley of *Assam* abound in gold, and this is in a manner corroborated by the numbers of the inhabitants of *Assam* who are gold-washers by profession; and judging from this fact, and the compacts which existed between the gold-washers and the state in regard to revenue payments, the quantity of gold received into the public treasury must have been considerable.

"The gold-washers of *Assam* are designated sonwals, but as they were distributed in different parts of the country, and placed under the authority of Phokans, Boorooahs, and other chiefs, they were generally known only by the names of the "Khel" or tribe of chief, under whom they resided. They were of all the classes and castes found in *Assam*, the Beheeahs (a tribe of Ahoms), and the Cassarees, being however the most numerous. The sonewahl Cassarees, who formerly occupied *Suddya* and its vicinity, were a distinct class from those residing, as before mentioned, under the orders and authority of different chiefs;

Miscellaneous.

Gold-washing.

they were entirely under the orders of the Rajah himself, and they supplied him with gold when called upon to do so.

"The whole of the rivers* in Assam contain (as formerly noticed) more or less gold in their sands, and the soil of which their banks are composed; the most noted, however, are the *Bor-oli*, *Subonshiri*, *Desue*, and *Joglo*, the two latter containing the purest and best gold; and in the *Joglo* it is said that this precious metal is found in large grains, about the size of a grain of rice. The colour of the gold, also, in both the last-named rivers is of a deep yellow, and it was so much prized, that the jewels of the Rajah's family of *Assam* were invariably made up on from what was collected in them.

"The gold of the *Bramahpootra* is considered the worst, and it seems to be a general opinion that the gold is best, and in greatest quantities, when the bed of the rivers is composed of a mixture of sand and small pebbles. I cannot, however, speak with confidence on this point, further than to observe, that the whole of the rivers I have enumerated have their sources in the mountains, and they have naturally for a considerable portion of their course a pebbly and stony bed.

"The *Desue* is a small river, and has sometimes little or no water in it; it has a short course from the mountains south of *Jorehaut* (where it

* A list has been given in the foregoing paper; but many names differ: Capt. H. states that, in fact, it comprehends all the rivers and torrent streams in *Assam*.

Miscellaneous.

rises) to the *Bramahpootra*, and a heavy shower of rain near its source causes it to rise suddenly. The gold-washers carry on their operations one and a half day's journey above *Jorehaut*, where the bed is stony.

Gold-washing.

"The *Joglo* rises in a range of small hills, which stretch across from *Jaipore* towards *Suddya*, and after a very short course of a few miles falls into the *Booree Dihing;* it has throughout a pebbly bed, and towards its mouth the banks are high and composed of yellow-coloured clay, similar to that of the hills and tract of country through which the *Joglo* passes. At the mouth of the last-named river the bed of the *Dihing* is conglomerate rock, rich in iron, and hills in which the *Joglo* has its rise, abound in iron and coal.

"The sonwals endeavour to keep their art as secret as possible, and wish to make people believe that they have particular methods of washing for gold, and that they alone know the most favorable spots for carrying on their operations. A few of these peculiarities, however, have been pointed out to me.

"The best time to wash for gold is after a rise of the waters in the rivers, and the most favorable spots are where beds of rivers are composed of small rounded pebbles of quartz and sandstone, with a mixture of sand, and also in spots where, from natural causes, there is an extensive deposit of this. In the *Joglo*, however, the soil is scraped from the banks, and washed, and I am told that the soil and sand which has collected about the roots of trees on the banks is considered rich in gold, but particularly when it has collected in considerable quantities round the fibrous roots of the gigantic fern. Miscellaneous. Gold-washing.

" Hollows and cavities in the loose ferruginous sandstone (which abounds in many of the rivers) are likewise cleared of all sand and gravel, the outer coating of the sandstone scraped off, and all is carefully washed. This last is said to be sometimes a prolific source of the precious metal.

" I have only twice witnessed the process of gold-washing, once in the *Irrawaddie* and once in the *Booree Dihing*, and although the method by the gold-washers differed, the soil washed was the same. The residue left, after the sand was washed out, was in both cases a black metallic looking sand, which contained the gold, and this blackish sand is invariably met with, excepting in washing the outer coating of the ferruginous sandstone above mentioned.*

"*Experiments.*—In the *Bramahpootra* or *Lohit*, which it is called above *Dibong Moukh*, and in the vicinity of *Tengapannee Moukh*, a party of Cassarees, sixty in number, washed for five days, and realized twenty-five rupees' weight

* Capt. H.'s account of the process and implements is omitted, as a tolerable description has already been given in the preceding paper. Might not the galvanic magnet be advantageously employed in freeing the washed sand of its ferruginous particles? We have frequently employed the common magnet in the examination of small specimens of these sands with advantage. The use of mercury might thus be avoided.

Miscellaneous.

Gold-washing.

of gold. Also twenty men for one month, who collected half a tolah, or eight rupees' worth of gold each. And fifteen men, for one month, collected each eight rupees' worth of gold. The above operations have been performed within the last few years.

"In the *Noa Dihing*, both above and below the present village of *Beesa*, a party of twenty Cassarees washed during three months, in the latter end of 1837, for gold, and realized eight annas weight each, in all ten tolahs, which was sold at *Syddya*, for twelve rupees per tolah of gold dust.

"In the *Booree Dihing*, a party of Cassaree traders in salt, twenty-four in number, washed for gold during their stay at *Jaipore* for one month, and realized in all twelve annas weight of gold.

"In the cases above mentioned there is a considerable difference in the quantities of gold collected. The last-named, however, being realized when the party were on a trading visit to *Jaipore* for salt, can hardly be considered as a fair specimen, as the washing for gold was looked upon more as a pastime, and the labour by no means constant. But the first-mentioned instance may be taken as a very fair specimen of what can be earned by gold-washing in the *Lohit*, when the numbers of the gold-washers are considerable, and when the object is to procure as much gold as they possibly can within a short period, which was the case in the instance above alluded to.

"The only peculiarity I can find worthy of notice, in regard to the foregoing information is, that in washing the sands of the *Noa Dihing*, a quantity of beautiful and minute crystals of quartz are left after the dirty portion and larger pieces of gravel have been thrown aside, and this description of residue is not observed in any other rivers of the upper portion of *Assam*. Miscellaneous. Gold-washing.

"I have also to remark that it is the custom with the sonwal Cassarees of *Suddya* to reckon four men to a gote, their method of washing for gold requiring for each durrunee, or trough, four men to keep the operation constantly going on, the distribution of them being one man to wash, two to bring the soil, and the fourth to dig—and all relieving each other at intervals.

"The information which is herein given may be depended upon as correct; it was taken from the head of a party of sonwal Cassarees, now residing at *Burgohain Pannee* on the south bank of the *Booree Dihing*, who make a yearly visit to the known sources of the precious metal. The dates are not specified, but the washing for gold took place at different periods.

"1. In the *Lohit* or *Bramahpootra* above *Suddya*, a party of gold-washers, consisting of twelve men, washed for twenty days, and realized seven tolahs of gold.

"2. In the *Dholjan* or A. B. *Bramahpootra*, a party of twenty men washed for sixteen days and realized one tolah.

Miscellaneous.

Gold-washing.

"3. In the *Jungi*, fifteen men washed for twenty days, and realized seven and a half tolahs.

"4. In the *Desue* or *Jorehaut* river, fifteen men washed for twelve days, and realized seven and a half tolahs.

"5. In the *Dhunseree* river, fifteen men washed for twelve or fifteen days, and realized seven and a half tolahs.

"With reference to the above, I have been told that the quantity of gold obtained in the three last-mentioned rivulets, or rather hill streams, may be taken as a good average of what can be procured from them; they are considered rich with reference to other streams in this province, which are washed for gold, and the quantity which could be obtained must depend upon the number of people employed. In my inquiries regarding particular localities, soil, &c. washed, I can obtain nothing additional to what I have already laid before you:—a sudden turn in the river where there is a deposit of loam sand and small round stones or pebbles, and a situation where the level of the country commences to ascend towards the hills, seem to be considered the most favorable localities with reference to the small streams which I have noticed here."

Captain Pemberton in his Report on the Eastern Frontier, page 82, says—

"Though most remarkable for the fertility of its alluvial soil, and variety of its products, Assam has been proved sufficiently rich in mineral treasures, to warrant the belief, that time only is required, to render them sources of national, as well as provincial, advantage. Almost all the streams which flow into the Burmahpootra are in a greater or less degree auriferous: the gold obtained at the junction of the Burmahpootra and Dhunseeree river alone, was estimated by Buchanan, in 1809, at one lakh and eighty thousand rupees per annum." Miscellaneous. Gold-washing.

SINCE closing this description of the Nagas, the arrival of a friend from that quarter has placed in the writer's hands, some memoranda which he had long considered to have been lost. The palm mentioned in page 40, as being found on the banks of the Boree Deehing, has been miscalled a *Cocos;* it being an undescribed species of *Areca*, bearing nuts of an oval form, small, and the substance of them diaphanous, with the streaks seen in the transverse section more regularly disposed in radii than are those of the common *betel* used by the natives of Bengal.

The white-blossomed Rhododendron which has of late been a good deal enquired about, is found, though rarely, on the Naga hills; being the *Rhododendron lepidotum* of Dr. Royle.

By the same opportunity, I also received a few zoological specimens, as some snakes, several of which are equally inhabitants of Lower Bengal, and a very fine new species of *Hyla*, or tree-frog, which, with some insects from the same quarter, have been deposited in the Asiatic Society's Museum. Among the recent additions to that Museum forwarded from Assam by Major Jenkins, I have seen two beautiful living jungle-cats, the *Felis bengalensis*, and *F. marmorata*, which latter is not enumerated in Dr. Walker's catalogue; and also a fine skull of a female Gaour (*Bos gaurus*) the so-called *Bison* of Indian sportsmen, being a very different animal from the *Methin* or Gayal, and which also is an addition to the catalogue of Assamese mammalia.

Note by William Griffith, Esq. M. D.

" The specimens of the fruit, used as Betel-nuts by the Nagas, communicated to the Agricultural Society, belong to an unpublished species of the genus *Areca*, which I call *Areca Nagensis*. From Mr. Owen's account it differs from all the Indian species of the same section of that genus by its tall, slender stature, and its being attached by innumerable coarse black roots : as it does in the fruit, spading, and size and shape of the fruits. An account of this species will appear in the December number of the Calcutta Journal of Natural History."

English.	Naga.
Fly, *n.*	mik cḥik
Fog	phu am
Follow	ka dí-ká ro
Fool	a pá
Foolish	a bá
Foot	dá
Forest	liŋ
Forget	i la-ko
Fork	káp
Frog	lúk
Fry	ŋó-o
Fruit	a rí
Full	chóŋ-e choŋ
Garden	pán
General	a haŋ
Get	i chú-o
Ginger	chiŋ
Girl	déhi ek cḥá
Give	kó-o
Glass	dá fá sók-tiŋ
Go	ká-o
Goat	ki en
God	Ka thak-raŋ
Gold	kam
Gong	jám
Good	a san
Goose	hán
Gown	khaṭ ṭók
Grass	hiŋ
Grass-hopper	kup cḥaŋ

English.	Naga.
Great	a-dóŋ
Green	a hiŋ
Greens	phe ru
Groan, *v.*	má chet rú-o
Grow	do-ŋo
Guava	madhú-riám
Gum	ŋe cḥá
Gun	van-tḥó
Hail	men
Hair	ka chó
Ham mer	jan wot-thiŋ
Hand	dak
Handkerchief	go-mo sa
Hard	a ché
Hare	ho há
Hat	ka fők
Hate	cḥin yá-o
Have	i tó-ŋa
Hawk	láh
He	a té
Head	khó
Hear	tá-to
Heavy	á lí
Heart	maŋ tó
Heaven	raŋ
Hell	no-rok
Hen	vó
Help	sá sye-to
Here	a naŋ
Heron	bú-gú li

English.	*Naga.*
Hew	chụ a-ko
Hide	rí a-mo
High	a chụ oŋ
Hill	há chóŋ
Hire, *n.*	a thá
Hit	sá há-po
Hog	vak
Hold	lu-o
Hole	a lo
Hoof	dá sók
Hook	ján phó-an
Hope	dá lam-mo
Horn	roŋ
Hornet	ŋyá máŋ kó
Horse	mók
Hot	a khám
Hour	dáṉr
House	hum
Howl	li-ŋo
Hunger	ram rí-o
Husband	de lá
I	ŋá
Idle	a jó
Immediately	dók-ko
In	hum nyu
Iron	ján
Island	chan-móŋ
Ivory	pu ok pá
Jackal	má bú
Jacket	cham-chóŋ
Jacktree	phan-dóŋ
Join	chó a-to
Joint	dak rik
Keep	ri e-mo
Key	hoŋ sát
Kill	rik vá-to
Kindle	tha-ko
King	chau fá
Kiss	tu-mo
Kite	láh
Knife	mit cha
Knee	dá-ku
Knock	a tuŋ ré-o
Knot	a sik
Know	i je-to
Ladder	hí-thó
Lady	ny oŋ
Lake	tham
Lamp	van-nán
Laugh	ŋi-o
Lazy	a jó
Law	ŋin chen
Lay	thi e-no
Lead, *v.*	shyet ká-to
Lead, *n.*	chún
Leaf	nyáp
Lean	à ràm
Leap	tu ó-ko
Leave	ti-no
Leech	sa vat

English.	*Naga.*
Left	hik
Leg	dà
Lend	nam kó o
Leopard	ru sà
Liar	mó thó-té
Lick	li ep da ko
Lie, *v.*	mó thó-o
Lift	tu o no
Light, *adj.*	à ré-sé
Light, *n.*	raŋ vó
Lightning	ki ep-dá
Lime	thun
Lion	hiŋ-kho
Little	a chà
Live	hi-ŋo
Lizard	chum-phó
Load, *n.*	pé
Look	syú-o
Loom	khát ták tiŋ
Long	á ló
Lord	phu-kon
Lose	má-phé o
Louse	rik
Love	riŋ cá-o
Low	a num
Lye	tap-jó
Mad	a pá
Maid	jan chó nyá
Maize	pó vóŋ
Man	mi-nyán
Mango	chu an ri ak
Many	á já
Market	hát
Marry	nam-la mo
Master	taŋ té
Mat	ham
Medicine	pham
Meet	í chu-o
Melt	pá kí-o
Mercy	húŋ
Middle	a móŋ
Midnight	pan móŋ
Milk	ŋiu-po
Minute	khon-tek
Mirror	dá fá sók-tin
Mix	lik sá-ko
Mock	ŋói-ko
Money	ŋun
Monkey	véh
Month	dá pe
Moon	dá
Morning	ran khá
Mother	íŋ-yóŋ
Mountain	há-hó
Mountaineer	sum-té
Mouse	jú-pu
Mouth	tun
Move	chó-o
Mud	bu ak ŋak
Musquito	maŋ-dóŋ

English.	*Naga.*	*English.*	*Naga.*
Mustard	hó ri oh	Other	a hán
Nail	go-jál	Overcome	jí e-no
Name	min	Owl	va-khú
Narrow	khá-riŋ	Ox	mán
Near	ther-kó	Paddy	chá
Neck	bó	Pair	á páŋ
Needle	mat kú	Palm, *tree*	tál-pát
Nest	á rúp	Pantaloons	dá-cḥamcḥóŋ
Net	cḥák	Paper	tu-lá pát
New	án-yán	Parrot	vá-kí
News	ŋin mat	Peach	mak-kho
Nice	a san-tham	Peacock	sói-jáŋ
Night	raŋ-pan	Pen	káp
No	má	Pepper	mak-phúp
Noise	nát-bá	Pigeon	pá-ri
Noon	pu ot-nyí	Pillow	kha-laŋ
North		Pinch	ti-ko
Nose	khó	Pineapple	há-pan dóŋ
Now	dok-ko	Pitcher	lu-tá
Oar	bo-thá	Place, *v.*	thí e-no
Obey	vé-o	Plain	há-túŋ
Officer	ká-phó	Plant, *v.*	khe-to
Oil	tán-thí	Plantain	ki e-ké
Old	a tó	Plough, *n.*	ná-ŋol
On	á khó-naŋ	Pointed	a ná
Onion	le-su on	Poison	bíh
Opium	ká-ni	Poppy	ká-ní baŋ
Open	já-no	Porcupine	ví khá
Orange	mú-thú lá	Post	thóŋ
Order, *n.*	ŋin	Pot	tik

Oi	oi	as in	*oi*l, bo*y*.
O'i	ói	„	sh*owy*.
Ou	ou	„	broader than *ou* in r*ou*nd.
Ph	ph	„	u*ph*old.
Rh	rh	„	pe*rh*aps.
Sh	sh	„	mi*sh*ap, di*sh*earten.
Sy	sy	„	rook'*s-y*ell, *sh*ell.
Th	th	„	pries*th*ood, (t dental.)
Ṭh	ṭh	„	ho*t-h*ouse.
Ui	ui	„	L*oui*siana.
U'i	úi	„	r*ui*n.
Zh	zh	„	jew*s-h*arp.
Zy	zy	„	pleasure [ple*z-y*ur], gla*zi*er.

VOCABULARY.

English.	*Naga.*	*English.*	*Naga.*
Above	á khó-naŋ	Ashes	tap lá
Ache, *v.*	cá-o	Ask	chye-no
Aged	té-ká	Ass	gá dho
Air	póŋ	Axe	vá-ká
Alike	a ró-raŋ	Back, *n.*	tam
All	phaŋ-taŋ	Bad	a chí
And	í ro ko vá	Bag	khaṭ ṭóŋ
Anger, *n.*	rin-khá	Ball	a kan
Ant	cip chak	Bamboo	vá
Arm	dak	Bark, *v.*	chó-ko
Arrive	i chú-o	Bark, *n.*	a khu on
Arrow	lát chán	Barrel	tham
Ascend	kó-o	Basket	ku oṉ-shí

English.	*Naga.*	*English.*	*Naga.*
Bason	káṉ-hi	Bone	á ráh
Bat	pha ka-raŋ	Book	ŋyáp raŋ
Bazar	ḣáṭ	Borrow	nam-mo
Be	dó-ŋo	Bow, *n.*	do ak háp
Bead	lik	Box	te-má
Bear, *n.*	sap-bá	Boy	na tá
Beat	vá-to	Bracelet	chán ká
Beautiful	a san-á	Branch	á phák
Bed	lí aŋ	Brass	pi-tol
Bee	ŋyá	Break	ŋu ak sye-to
Beg	chu-o	Breast	tan khú
Believe	pú té-o	Bridge	síh
Bell	cáŋ shí	Bring	van-ro
Belly	vók	Broad	khá-dóŋ
Bend	nu-o	Brook	ju on cḥá
Betelnut	ka vé	Broom	vá-me ló ap
Bind	kha-ko	Brother	í phó
Bird	vó	„ (younger)	í náh
Bite, *v.*	ka-ko	Bruise, *v.*	phí eŋ sye-to
Bitter	a khá	Brush, *n.*	cḥóh
Black	an yak	Buffalo	lé
Blanket	khaṭ-dóŋ	Bug	cip-sá
Blind	mit du ok	Build	hu o no
Blood	hé	Burn, *v.*	tha ko
Blow, *v.*	maṭ-to	Bury	bi-no
Blue	á ham	Butterfly	phán-phe
Board	pan cḥu ok	Buy	rí-o
Boat	khu oṉ-khó	Call, *v.*	ru-o
Body	sak	Candle	ŋyáso van-án
Boil	pha-to	Cannon	van-tó dóŋ

English.	Naga.	English.	Naga.
Cap	ka fók	Copper	tám
Carry	kap ká-to	Cotton	ko-páh
Cart	roth	Cough, *v.*	cho-ko
Caste	kul	Country	há dáŋ
Cat	mi aŋ	Cover, *n.*	ká-hap
Catch	lu-o	Cow	mán
Caterpillar	chú	Crab	sán
Chaff	vi ak	Creek	ju on chá
Chain	ján rú	Creep	khu o-mo
Chair	tóŋ tiŋ	Crest	khu ó thu op
Cheek	than	Crocodile	ghóŋ-ri al
Chest	pe-rá	Crooked	a-ku aŋ
Chew	sau-o	Crow, *n.*	vak há
Child	na tá	Cry, *v.*	sa-po
Chin	ká	Cu bit	dak-ká
Chisel	se	Cup	bán chạ́
Choose	ran-no	Curry	phe rú
City	pàn kú on	Curtain	á thu á
Citron	chạ́ chó	Cut, *v.*	du a-ko
Cloth	khaṭ	Dance, *v.*	ru-o
Clothes	kha ṭa khú	Dark	raŋ-ŋyak
Cloud	phu am	Daughter	dé hi ek-chá
Coal	van hi	Day	raŋ ŋyí
Cock's comb	à su oŋ	Deaf	ná-bá
Cocoanut	nà-ri kol	Dear	thá chán
Cold	akí	Deep	a lú
Comb, *n.*	chọ́	Deer	ké hé
Come	ká-ro	Delay, *v.*	ba-mo
Command, *v.*	ri-ŋi to	Demon	jó bán
Cook, *v.*	pu o-no	Deny	sá-o

English.	*Naga.*	*English.*	*Naga.*
Descend	já-o	End	a ráh
Dew	bin-ti	Enter	lú-pi ko
Die	rí-o	Evening	raŋ já
Dig	thu-o	Eye	mit
Dip	chá-mo	Face	than
Dirt	bum	Fair	paŋ-san
Do	ré-o	Fall	i já-o
Dog	hú	Fan	jam-lap
Dove	phók fé-te rú	Far	há ló
Drag	luaŋsye-to	Fat	a tat
Draw	sye-to	Father	vá
Dream, *n.*	mat-maŋ	Fear, *v.*	ché-o
Drink	jó ko	Feather	nap
Drive	jun lú-o	Feel	lam pu ó-mo
Dry, *v.*	chu ok la-mo	Fence	pàn
Duck	pàk màk	Fever	a chàt
Dull	a tók	Few	a né
Dumb	a bá	Field	pít
Eagle	laŋ-tàŋ	Fight	ràn man no
Ear	ná	Fill	sa-ko
Earknob	ná-thó	Find	i chu-o
Ear (of corn)	a chóŋ	Finger	dak-sú
Early	mà mà	Fire	van
Earth	há	Fish	ŋá
East	sán hóŋ	Flat	to-de
Eat	chá-o	Flesh	ŋam
Egg	a tí	Float	lú om phó-o
Elbow	dak kú	Floor	vá-lam
Elephant	pu ok	Flower	chóŋ po
Empty	á hó-tá	Fly, *v.*	pú-o

APPENDIX;

CONTAINING

A KEY TO THE PRONUNCIATION;

WITH

A VOCABULARY AND READING LESSONS,

OF THE

NAGA LANGUAGE.

THE NAGA LANGUAGE.

Key to the Pronunciation.

Rom.	*Let.*	*Names.*	*Sounded as in*
A	a	a	*A*meric*a*, s*u*mm*e*r.
A'	á	á	f*a*r, f*a*ther.
B	b	bí	*b*ut.
C	c	cí	chip, (*ts.*)
D	d	dí	spen*d*thrift, (soft dental d.)
Ḍ	ḍ	ḍí	*d*eed, (hard d.)
E	e	e	m*e*n, also *e* in th*e*re.
E'	é	é	th*ey*, s*ay*.
F	f	ef	*f*ame.
G	g	gé	*g*o, *g*un.
H	h	hé	*h*ave.
Ḥ	ḥ	ḥé	*h*ouse (hard guttural h.)
I	i	i	p*i*n, p*i*ty.
I'	í	í	pol*i*ce, f*ee*l.
J	j	jé	*j*ewel, (nearly as *dz.*)
K	k	ké	*k*ing.
L	l	el	*l*and.
M	m	em	*m*an.
N	n	en	*n*oon.
Ñ	ṉ	eṉ	e*n*fa*n*t (French.)
Ṇ	ŋ	eŋ	si*ng*i*ng*, spri*ng*.
O	o	o	l*o*rd, l*aw*, also *o* in n*o*t.
O'	ó	ó	n*o*te, r*o*be.

Rom.	*Let.*	*Names.*	*Sounded as in*
P	p	pí	*p*ine-a*pp*le.
R	r	ár	*r*oll, *r*ewa*r*d.
S	s	es	*s*entence.
T	t	tí	Ma*t*-thew, eigh*t*-th (dental t.)
Ṭ	ṭ	ṭí	*t*en*t* (hard t.)
U	u	u	b*u*ll, book.
U'	ú	ú	r*u*le, sch*oo*l.
V	v	ví	*v*ine.
W	w	wí	*w*ish, *w*ant.
Y	y	yí	*y*outh, *y*eoman.
Z	z	zí	*z*eal, i*s*.

Fundamental Rule. In combinations, every letter has the same sound as when used singly.

Ai	ai	as in	*ai*sle, pine.
A'i	ái	„	*ay*.
Au	au	„	round, no*w*.
A'u	áu	„	ho*w*l, (sound protracted.)
Bh	bh	„	a*bh*or.
Ch	ch	„	har*tsh*orn.
Dh	dh	„	a*dh*ere, (dental d.)
Ḍh	ḍh	„	chil*dh*ood.
Ei	ei	nearly as *i* in pine, but more close.	
Eu	eu	resembling *ou* in r*ou*nd, (closer than au.)	
Gh	gh	as in	Le*gh*orn.
Iu	iu	„	artic*u*late.
Iú	iú	„	p*u*re, n*ew*.
Jh	jh	„	he*dg*e-*h*og.
Kh	kh	„	wor*k*-*h*ouse.
Ny	ny	„	Bu*ny*an.

English.	*Naga.*	*English.*	*Naga.*
Potato	há khu on	Rhinoceros	gonr
Pour	ki e-no	Rice	vóŋ
Powder	khár	Right	cḥá
Pray	raŋ thá-mo	Ring	khap
Press	thi-ŋo	Ripe	á chúm
Pull	sye-to	Rise, *v.*	cha-po
Pumpkin	kum	River	jó-an
Push	thu a-mo	Road	lam
Put	thi e-no	Roar	li-ŋo
Quail	vo-phút	Roast	há-ŋo
Quarrel, *v.*	ma-no	Roll	lu a-ŋo
Queen	vaŋ cḥá	Roof	sḥúp
Quick	kho rók	Root	a riŋ
Raft	vó-at	Rope	rú
Rain	raŋ-pát	Rotten	á sán
Rake	ja-bó ká	Round	á túm
Rainbow	cḥán-cḥu on	Rub, *v.*	hú-to
Raise	tu o-no	Rum	lo-ru
Rat	jú pu	Run, *v.*	cḥu a-no
Ratan	rí	Rust	chin
Raven	va-khá	Saddle	do-li sá
Razor	kho cḥún nit	Salt, *n.*	súm
Read	vé-o	Salt, *adj.*	sum-khá
Reap	kha-no	Sand	se
Receive	tá-o	Saucy	ŋin-dóŋ
Red	a cḥak	Save	sá-sye to
Religion	dho rom	Saw, *n.*	ko-rot
Remain	ba-mo	Say	thó-o
Remember	hú-no	Scab	a kḥu ap
Rest, *v.*	bó an tó-ŋo	Scales	tu ok chá

English.	Naga.
Scholar	phó li kap
Scissors	ká-ṭi
Scold	khá-o
Scorch	sá-po
Scrape	hí e-to
Screw	pe̲n̲s
Scriptures	hás-tro
Sea	jó-dóŋ
See	khé-o
Seed	a kan
Seek	la mo
Sell	sa-ŋo
Send	háp-phé o
Serve	khà-ti o
Sew	phi-ŋo
Shadow	raŋ bin
Shake	mót-sye to
Shame, *v.*	ré sé-o
Shape, *n,*	raŋ raŋ-á
Sharp	a ná
Sheep	khi en
Shell	pàk-màk
Shield	lák
Shine	cḥú-mo
Ship	já háj
Shoes	poi-jár
Short	a tó-on
Shoulder	cḥu a-kḥó
Shove	tup phye-to
Show	khé-sa ko

English.	Naga.
Shoot	há-po
Shun	thi-ŋo
Shut	sa-ko
Sick	á cḥat
Side	á chám
Sieve	jún-phá
Sign	a mán
Silkworm	mú ga dóŋ
Silver	ŋún
Sin	páp
Sing	sé-sé o
Sink	lúm-já o
Sister	íŋ-yáh
Sit	tó-ŋo
Skin	á khu on
Sky	ráŋ tuŋ hává
Slant	ku óŋ ké
Slap	átaŋková-to
Slave	í há
Sleep, *v.*	jú-po
Sleep, *n.*	júp-mat
Slide	anyenkhono
Slow	a ré
Small	á riŋ
Smell, *v.*	kí-no
Smile, *v.*	ŋé-o
Smith	ko-már
Smoke.	van khú
Smooth	án-yen
Snake	pú

English.	*Naga.*	*English.*	*Naga.*
Sneeze	kó-khi ko	Stag	chók
Snore	kó-ro-o	Stab	su-o
Snow	mí-en	Stand	cḥa po
Soft	án-yen	Star	mé-rik
Soldier	rán-ṭé	Steal	hú-o
Son	cḥá	Steel	ná-thi
Some	khá-té	Stem	á kóŋ
Soul	dá-fá	Stone	lon
Sound	a ró-raŋ	Stoop	ku-no
Sour	á sí	Stop	ba-mo
South		Straight	á tiŋ
Sow, *v.*	va-no	Stretch	syé-to
Spade	ján-van	Strike	vá-to
Sparrow	va sáŋ sik	String	rú
Speak	thó-o	Strong	á cḥán
Spear	pá	Stump	thóŋ-khó
Spider	mák cḥáŋ	Such	a ró-raŋ
Spill	phé-o	Sugar	sí-ni
Spin	phu-o no	Sugar-cane	tho-mu
Split	khau-o	Sun	sán
Spoon	heṉ-tá	Swap	li-ko
Spread	la-mo	Swear	tuamhó-no
Spring, *n.*	jó mik	Sweat, *n.*	ráŋ-lam
Spring, *v.*	dantuo-ko	Sweep	mé-o
Sprinkle, *v.*	sho-ṭ i o	Sweet	á tú
Sprout, *n.*	á chóŋ	Swell, *v.*	phi-ŋo
Spur	a kin	Swift	ko rók
Squeeze	phye-to	Swim	á juk-ri o
Squir rel	cḥen-cḥa	Sword	daŋ-ló
Staff	la khú-ti	Table	khu áŋ-fáŋ

English.	*Naga.*	*English.*	*Naga.*
Tail	á mé	Tongue	tha lí
Take	ka-po	Tooth	pá
Tamarind	te-lé li	Top	a ráh
Tea	phá lap	Touch, *v.*	mó a-ko
Teacher	hé tó te	Tree	baŋ
Tear, *v.*	kha-sẹhe to	True	á liŋ
Tear, *n.*	mit-phí	Turban	khó-dik
Tell	ŋá-o	Turn	phó-no
Tent	khat-húm	Turtle	khó-kap
That	í-ra pá	Tusk	pá-dóŋ
They	se niŋ	Twig	á phák
Thief	a hú	Twin	chạá pi et
Thigh	vé-róŋ	Twist, *v.*	phu ó-no
Thin	a chạá	Ugly	paŋ-cí
Think	hu no	Umbrella	khat-húp
This	a-rá pá	Uncle	dí-dí
Thou	maŋ-má	Under	a khan
Thorn	sú	Understand	í ja-to
Thread	rí	Unripe	á hiŋ
Throat	bo	Valley	jóŋ
Throw	pa-tó	Village	há
Thumb	dak-shu	Vine	rú
Thunder	ráŋ mók	Vomit	phát phé-o
Tiger	sá	Vulture	láŋ-táŋ
Time	sán	Waistcloth	ka rí
Toad	luk	Wait	má-o
Tobacco	van-khú	Wake	chi-ŋo
To-day	ta já	Walk	khu a-mo
Toe	dá shu	Want	í la-mo
To-morrów	ni-nap	War	rán

English.	Naga.	English.	Naga.
Warm	á khám	Wind, *n*.	póŋ
Wash, *v*.	su a-no	Wing	á raŋ
Watch, *v*.	ta-ŋo	Wipe	hu tó
Water	jó	Wise	húŋ te
Wax	nyá-só	Wish, *v*.	chu-o
We	ní ma	Wolf	só-an
Weak	á chán-a hó	Woman	dé hi ek
Wear	thó-ko	Wood	pan
Widow	ján té ŋyú	Word	ŋin
Widower	ján té vá	Work, *v*.	mó ot mó-o
Weave	ta-ko	Work, *n*.	mó-ot
Well, *n*.	nád	World	há háŋ
Weigh	tu a-ko	Worm	dóŋ
West	sán-yap	Worship, *v*.	su á-mo
What	che-ná	Wring	ra-po
Wheel	ghi-lá	Yam	há-khu on
Where	mo kó-á	Year	raŋ pá
Whet	má-no	Yell, *v*.	ra-ko
Whisper	fú fúfá fá-o	Yellow	á mi en
Whistle, *v*.	sí si su a-ko	Yes	i dá ŋá
White	a pó	Yesterday	ma já
Which	ma pá	Yoke	ju o-li
Who	ha-ná	You	né-má
Wife	taŋ ŋyú	Young	á ti en
Wild	á phá	Youth	jan-chó
Wind, *v*.	dap-thi e no		

EASY READING LESSONS.

English.	*Naga.*
He cannot come.	Tá ká-má rá.
It will rain.	Raŋ ipá-thá.
Bring an umbrella.	Khat-húp van-ro.
A dá is wanting.	Daŋ ván-the ila-me.
Take that away.	Apá kap ká-to.
A foreign ship has arrived.	Firi-ŋe khuon-khó adóŋ-láhu-thá.
The village is distant.	Há aló.
The elephant roars.	Puok ali-ŋiká.
The rat gnaws.	Jú-pumá phá-kitá.
The fire burns.	Van-má khá-mitá.
What is he seeking?	Cḥen lam sú-ito?
The boy plays.	Natá luó-miká.
Where is the cat?	Miaŋ makó itó-ŋa?
William is a good boy.	Wil-yam natá ásan.
He came from Europe.	Yú-rop ková ipá vaŋ-thá.
I have learned nineteen letters.	Icḥi ván-ikhú á-khor hé-tak.
A foolish boy cannot learn.	Abá natá-pá jenhé-má.
The teacher calls.	Hikai-temá rú-itá.
A ruler gives commands.	Até-sómá chie-nitá.
The water boils.	Jó pha-tiká.
The sun is very hot.	Sán-má laŋ-má sai-haŋ.
The centipede has many legs.	Pútamté-suon adá ájá.

English.	*Naga.*
A sword is sharp.	Daŋ aló áná.
The mouse runs.	Jú-pu cuó niká.
Z is the last letter.	Zí á-khor kadí-maŋ.
The lion is king over all beasts. The elephant is great. An elephant has four legs. He has broad ears, and a long trunk. He will strike you with his trunk.	Phaŋ-taŋ ké-hé tokko, hiŋ-kho chaufá. Puok adóŋ. Puok adá ká-bili. Aná khá-doŋ, asebe áló. Asebe púŋma naŋ-naŋ iváthá.
A man has two hands, and two feet. The eagle is king over birds. The dog barks. A jackal carried off three fowls at night. Give a gun; I will go and shoot him.	Mi-nyán adak ká-nyí, adá ká-nyí. Pháŋ-taŋ vó tók-ko, láŋtáŋ chaufá. Hú-má ichó-ká. Mábúma ta-pan vó ván-ram lákáta. Van-thó ván-the kó-o; ŋá-má há-paŋ.
A horse has long legs, and a long neck. He can run fast. Do you not wish to get upon his back? Do not strike him. Hold fast; if you do not hold, you will fall.	Mók dá áló; ábó áló. Khorók itá chuo-ná. A tam-konaŋ chaŋ-aŋ naŋ ai tó á? Até-naŋ nak váto. Achán-má lú-o. Na lú-koko ajá iré-o.
That goat has two kids. She gives good milk. The cow gives milk. The dog has four legs, and two ears.	Ira kien nyóŋ-pá achá vá nyi itó-ŋá. Niu-po asan raŋ kó-hi. Mánnyóŋ ŋiu-po raŋ kó-hi. Hú dá ká bilí, aná kányí.

English.	*Naga.*
The hog is very cross. He thrusts his nose into the mud.	Vak alaŋ jo. A´túnpá buakŋak khan-naŋ saktie-nitá.
The tiger kills men. The rhinoceros has one horn.	Sá má mi-nyánhé rik ika-ká. Gon̲r aróŋ vánthe itó-ŋá.
The cat will catch mice. She can see in the dark. Giver her milk. Do not pull her tail. If you pull her tail she will scratch you· Her nails are sharp.	Miaŋ-má jú-pu ilu-á. Raŋ ŋyak-naŋ até-má icḥam ikhé-á. A´té-naŋ ŋiu-po kó-o. Até ámé-naŋ nak sye-to. A´ménaŋ masye-toko, aphúk syét iré-á Até dak-hin aná.
See that fine fish I caught it with a hook. It is not dead. It shakes its tail. Without water, it will not live. Men cannot live in water.	I´ra ŋá san-pá syú-o. Ná-má jánphóan-má lá-ló-tak. Má rí-ká; ámé-ran muó-ṭá. Jó áhó-oko hin má. Mì-nyán jó-naŋ atá hiŋ má-
Here is a great snake.	Pú adóŋ itó-ŋá.
Do you not hear that bird sing? She has lit upon that tree. Do not steal her eggs. If you steal her eggs, she will cry all the day. So doing, you will be a bad boy.	I´ra vó ruot-pá tát-má tó-ne? Baŋ kho-naŋ pai-ká. Atí-pá naŋ-má nak hú-o. Atí-pá naŋ-má ma-hú-oko, ŋítaŋ isa-pá I´ru okote, naŋ natá san-má.

English.	*Naga.*
It rains. It thunders. See the lightning! Are you not afraid? If you are a good boy, you need not fear. God will take care of you.	Raŋ pát ké-rá Raŋ mú-khiká. Kiep-dá syú-o! Naŋ ché mó ne? Natá asan madaŋ okote, aché tiŋ daŋ-ná. Katak-raŋ ipá-má.
Bring me that book. Where did you get it? I bought it for a hiki. I shall soon read it. Take care, do not wet it.	I'ra ŋyápráŋ-pá itá-naŋ van-ro. Naŋ manaŋ-vá chó-tó? Ná-má hik-i van-the kó-lakmá, rí-tak. Khorók itá já-paŋ. Syú-o, nak sán phé-o.
William is a good boy. He learns fast. When he is not reading, he works. He does not say, *I cannot.* He will be a great man. He will be rich.	Wil-yam natá asan. Nyá-raŋ ije-thá. Ne hé-koko móot imó-á. *Tá-mak ŋá-má* thó má. Até mi-nyán adóŋ idá-ŋá; et-chu idá-ŋá.
That boy is lazy. He cannot read, He never works. His clothes are very dirty and ragged. He has no money. Where will he get food? A lazy boy can never be rich.	I'ra natá-pá ajó dé-ká. Nyáp-ráŋ tá jáp má. Até-má matú-omin móot mó-má. Até khat-pá mak ajá, kachen karien dé.ká. Até ŋun ahó-tú. Cham makó ichó-á? Ajó natá-pá matú-omin té-chu dáŋ-má.
Samuel, where have you been? I have been to school. For what purpose did you go? I went to learn to read.	Sámuel, naŋ manaŋ ká-tó? Phólí-raŋ hum-naŋ ká-tak. Chen ré-ráŋ ká tó-á? A'jáp-róŋ, ajet-ráŋ ká-tak.

English.	*Naga.*
Do you not play at school? I do not play much. Once or twice I whispered and laughed. That is bad. Play at home; having come to school keep silent.	Phólí-raŋ hum-naŋ taŋ-tú-oko, luó-má tó ne? Ájyá-te luó-mak; lik-the, lik ni fú-fú fá-fá ŋyé-kaŋ. San má; ma húm-naŋ luó-mo; phóli-ráŋ hum-naŋ ma-ká-roko, nak-ti nú-o.
Sir, Thomas has struck me. Why did you strike him? I did not strike him; he pinched me. Do not lie. You struck him, did you not? Yes, sir. Thomas, you have told a lie. I must punish you. Bring a rod.	Sá-háb, Tho-mas ŋá-naŋ lává-thaŋ. Até-naŋ cḥeráŋ vá-tho? Ná-má vá-tho va; até-má ŋá-naŋ atikré-taŋ. Mó thó ŋin nak thó-o. Naŋ-má até-naŋ vá-thó ne? Sá-háb idá-ŋá. Tho-mas naŋ mó-thó thó-tó. Naŋ-naŋ ŋá-má vá-thiŋ. Sá-but la-the van-ro.
Do not tell lies. If you tell lies, you will be a bad boy. Do not steal. If you steal, God will see you.	Mó thó, nak thó-o. Mó thó thó-te, natá acḥi; san-má. Nak hú o. Mahú-oko Katak-raŋmá ikhé-a.
You must not drink rum, nor eat opium. If you drink rum, and eat opium, when you have grown up, you will be a bad man. A bad man who steals, tells lies, and disobeys God, will go to hell.	Lo-ru, ne ká-ni jók ápien. Lo-ru, ne ká-ni majó-koko, kadí-naŋ madóŋ-oko, mi-nyán acḥí ida-ŋá. Mi-nyán acḥí, han-má mahú-oko, mó thó meré-oko. Raŋka-tak-raŋnaŋ amiŋ vé-má-no-rok-naŋ iva-ŋá.

English.	*Naga.*
There is one God, by name Jehovah. There is no other God. This God built the heavens. He created the earth. He made me, you, and all men. He made the green tree, the high mountain, the great sea, the sun, the moon, and the shining stars. He sees in all places. As he sees in light, so he sees in darkness. Whatever you do he perfectly understands. Take heed therefore not to sin.	Katak-raŋ ván-the itó-ŋá; írá min-pá Yihó-vá. Katak-raŋ ahán ahó. Íra Katak-raŋpá raŋ tiek-tá. Ate-má ha-min tiek-tá. Ná-naŋ, naŋ-naŋ, hué-ri mi-nyánnaŋ tiek-tá. Baŋ áhiŋ, há hó acúoŋ, jó adoŋ, sán, dá-fe, mérik achúm, ti ek-tá. Phaŋ, taŋ lát-naŋ ekhé-á. Raŋvo-naŋ maró ekhé-á, raŋ-ŋyak, naŋ min iró ikhé-á, Naŋmá chẹn ré á-komin, até phaŋ-taŋ ije-tá. Naŋ iróko mat, nak kapthaŋ-má, ŋya-raŋ syú-o.
The hearts of all men are evil. Without new hearts, they will fall into hell. Who can give a new heart? God alone. Beside him, no one can give it.	Hué-re mi-nyánre riŋ achị́. Riŋ anyán na chó-koko, no-roknaŋ ijá. Riŋ anyán han-má itá kó-á? Katak-raŋ alak-lak. Írokó-và han-má min itá kó-á.
Who can remove your sin? Jesus Christ, the Son of God, can remove it. He has given his own body to be wounded and slain, that wicked men might live.	Maraŋ thup han-má itá máphé-á? Katak-raŋ Icḥá-má, Yé-shú Khristemá, itá máphé-á. Matvá mí hiŋ-ràŋ, asak phuoŋ-pá, avan-ráŋ, avat-raŋ thá-itá.
Therefore pray unto him; he will hear. Although he	Íroko até-naŋ ruó-lómá suá-mo; até-máitá tá. Ácu-

English.	*Naga.*
is far off in the high heavens, he can hear whatever you say.	oŋ raŋ-naŋ áté meratho háló a-komin, naŋ-má cḥen cḥen matú-oko ìcham itá-tá.

NUMERALS.

1	vánthe	30	ruak ram
2	ványí	40	ruak belí
3	vánram	50	ruak baŋá
4	belí	60	ruak írók
5	baŋá	70	ruak íŋit
6	írók	80	ruak ísat
7	íŋit	90	ruak íkhú
8	ísat	100	cḥá-the
9	íkhú	200	cḥá nyí
10	íchi	300	cḥá ram
11	íchi vánthe	400	cḥá belí
12	íchi ványí	500	cḥá baŋá
13	íchi vánram	600	cḥá írók
14	íchi vánbelí	700	cḥá íŋit
15	íchi vánbaŋá	800	cḥá ísat
16	íchi vánírók	900	cḥá íkhú
17	íchi váníŋit	1000	cḥá íchi
18	íchi vánísat	10,000	hájat íchi
19	íchi váníkhú	1,000,000	hájat cḥáthe
20	ruak ŋí		